What they are saying about IGNITE

'I don't believe there's anything more important we could give ourselves to than raising up radical disciples for Jesus. That's why I'm so delighted that Big Ideas are attempting to do this through their brilliant new IGNITE resources.'

Andy Hawthorne (*The Message*)

'There is an enormous need for training in discipleship. Equally, there is an enormous leakage of young people from the churches. You are taking trouble over both.'

Rev. Michael Green

'Coming to faith is one thing, living the faith we've found to the full is another. I believe IGNITE to be a launch pad for that exciting journey of discipleship. It's radical, it's relevant and I commend it to you.

John Glass (General Superintendent, Elim Pentecostal Churches)

'Once in a while you stumble across something you believe God could use to transorm lives – the IGNITE declaration project is just one of those God-given ideas that will make a difference. I commend Big Ideas for taking this initiative.'

Jonathan Booth (Director – Care for the Family)

'IGNITE – another great idea – may it truly strike a light for a time such as this.'

J. John (The Philo Trust)

ignite

God's Purpose for This Generation

NIGEL JAMES

survivor

ISBN 1 84291 050 7

Published by
KINGSWAY COMMUNICATIONS LTD
Lottbridge Drove, Eastbourne, BN23 6NT, England.
Email: books@kingsway.co.uk

Book design and production for the publishers by
Bookprint Creative Services, P.O. Box 827, BN21 3YJ, England.
Printed in Great Britain.

contents

foreword

In October of 2000, I was travelling through Britain and parts of Europe on my Transform Tour. One of our concert stops was in Cardiff, which will for ever be logged very firmly in my memory. It was a rather memorable night for two very different reasons. First because my all-time most embarrassing stage moment occurred that night (and yes, I must leave it up to your imagination and the remembrance of those who were there!). But the second, more important, reason for that night being memorable for me was because I heard for the first time about IGNITE. I even signed a wallet-sized card saying that I would commit to the six points of the IGNITE declaration. In my concerts I have my own five points encouraging people to pray, read the Bible, have Christian accountability, get rid of junk and be involved in a strong church family. So I strongly believe in the essence of this book. We all need reminders like the IGNITE declaration to spur us on.

Also, I appreciate Nigel's obvious passion to see youth and adults discipled and plugged into God. I encourage you to read this book and take very seriously the challenges it holds. God calls us all to absolute commitment and a radical love of Him and others. Let's get to it!

> So here's what I want you to do, God helping you: Take your everyday, ordinary life – your sleeping, eating, going-to-work, and walking-around life – and place it before God as an offering . . . Don't become so well-adjusted to your culture that you fit into it without even thinking. Instead, fix your attention on God. You'll be changed from the inside out. (Romans 12, *The Message*)

All for God,
Rebecca St James

1

start here

I grew up in the church and kept on going throughout my teenage years. Exciting activities and good friends were the reasons I stayed involved, but because I kept going I did discover Jesus. I can vividly remember lying in bed one night when my old valve radio set had blown up, and instead of listening to Radio Luxembourg (this was the mid 1970s) my mind drifted onto being a Christian. Quite simply I decided I was going to live my life for Jesus, and initially thought that meant being a minister in the church.

For the rest of my teenage years and into my twenties I was a committed and outspoken Christian, but no one took the time to go through the basics of Christian living with me. The church I grew up in was strong socially but never equipped me practically for real life.

My heart and mind said that I was a Christian but my lifestyle and actions screamed otherwise.

Consequently by the time I got to university I was leading a double life – my Christian faith on the one hand, and the same typical lifestyle of partying, sport, debt and promiscuity that so often accompanies student existence on the other. I would tumble into bed after an all-night party just in time to snatch a couple of hours' sleep before church, and was often torn between the Christian Union Bible study and going partying with my girlfriend, who wasn't a Christian. My beliefs had no solid foundation to be based on and little to challenge me to a lifestyle of discipleship. My poor attempts at witnessing were completely compromised by the way I chose to live my life. Deep down I knew the mess I was in but it took a good few years before I let God deal with me.

Now, over 20 years later, I meet young Christians faced with some of the same struggles. At the same time I see a generation of Christians faced with new issues – an attitude of consumerism that affects the way they view church and Christian culture, and a complacency and comfort about their own Christian life that sometimes prevents them looking to the lost. At the other end of the spectrum to the church I grew up in, I still see churches so preoccupied in 'decisions', 'commitments', and 'saving' people that they give the impression initial faith in Jesus is the end of the story, not the beginning. And I'm an evangelist, remember, so I love seeing people come to faith!

IGNITE has grown out of a desire to see young people accept the challenge to find God's purpose in their lives and to lead a life of radical discipleship. It's also grown out of a personal desire to help young people avoid the mistakes I made. The heart of the IGNITE declaration is nothing new; in fact it's simply putting biblical principles into a format that can captivate and strengthen an emerging generation so that they can become a model for their non-Christian peers and for the wider church.

Let me explain what I'm going on about by giving you an illustration. Uncle Donald and Auntie Sheila are relatives of Gill, my wife. They are some of our favourite people. They live in Eastbourne and sometimes take all day to travel in their car to visit us in Cardiff – a journey that could be done in four hours. I've always had a joke with them about how slowly they drive: on their honeymoon back in the 1960s they apparently travelled on a scooter from London to Cornwall for a week's holiday. I reckon they took three days to get there and three days to get back! Their retort to me is always that they like to enjoy the journey, stopping off at scenic spots, having a cup of coffee and enjoying each other's company. When I drive, I just want to get from A to B as soon as is legally possible, regardless of what I pass on the way.

The more I discover about Christianity, the more I realise it is a journey. If our sights are purely set on heaven as our destination, with little regard for the places we will travel on our way, then I believe we fail to be the people God wants us to be. What God desires is people who after conversion will be equipped, encouraged and challenged to make the most of their journey and embrace it with everything they have got. God wants travellers like Donald and Sheila, not like me! We have got to start taking the journey itself as seriously as we take the starting point and the destination.

A valid definition of disciple could be 'follower'; this book will help you discover that the type of person who takes up the challenge of igniting a passion for Jesus in their life will be someone who:

- follows Jesus
- follows Him closely
- meets other followers
- travels with other followers
- wants more people to join the journey
- is always excited about better ways to travel

It's this travel guide that is at the centre of IGNITE. Each one of the above travel tips has been expanded and encapsulated in the IGNITE declaration:

IGNITE

I believe that God has a special purpose for my generation and me. I ask God to IGNITE in me a desire to discover this purpose.

I commit to:

Include Jesus in my moral life, my thoughts, words, actions and relationships.

Grow closer to Jesus through studying the Bible, praying and allowing the Holy Spirit to lead me each day.

Network with other Christians in my city, my country and throughout the world.

Involve myself in a local church and respect its leadership.

Take the message of Jesus into my school, college or place of work and the world by praying, living and witnessing so that everyone may have an opportunity to know Jesus.

Explore God's will for myself and my generation and seek to follow it.

Why the name IGNITE?

I hope the word IGNITE conjures up for you the image of fire, of flames, of extreme temperature. The Bible is full of imagery about fire, especially the fire of God. At various times the word 'fire' is used to describe the glory of God, His presence and protection, His holiness, His anger against sin and His righteousness and judgement. In other instances 'fire' represents the Holy Spirit, the inspiration that a prophet has, and the particular religious feeling a person has.

Just look at some of the ways fire is described in the book of Jeremiah for instance:

They have lied about the LORD; they said, 'He will do nothing! No harm will come to us; we will never see sword or famine. The prophets are but wind and the word is not in them; so let what they say be done to them.' Therefore this is what the LORD God Almighty says: 'Because the people have spoken these words, I will make my words in your mouth a fire and these people the wood it consumes.' (Jeremiah 5:12–14)

O my people, put on sackcloth and roll in ashes; mourn with bitter wailing as for an only son, for suddenly the destroyer will come upon us. 'I have made you a tester of metals and my people the ore, that you may observe and test their ways. They are all hardened rebels, going about to slander. They are bronze and iron; they all act corruptly.

The bellows blow fiercely to burn away the lead with fire, but the refining goes on in vain; the wicked are not purged out. They are called rejected silver, because the LORD has rejected them.' (Jeremiah 6:26–30)

In the next chapter we'll discover about God's consuming fire and His refining fire as seen in the above verses. The fire of God can also be seen in Scripture to represent punishment and destruction:

But if you do not obey me to keep the Sabbath day holy by not carrying any load as you come through the gates of Jerusalem on the Sabbath day, then I will kindle an unquenchable fire in the gates of Jerusalem that will consume her fortresses. (Jeremiah 17:27)

However, above all IGNITE should conjure up the image of being so on fire for Jesus that you can't help but spontaneously combust because of the extreme passion and commitment you display when God ignites your life. It's unquenchable! The Hebrew and Greek words used in the original texts for 'fire' actually mean the state of something catching alight and combusting and the signs that can be seen from that – flames for example. So IGNITE is about not just being on fire but being seen to be on fire! Listen to Jeremiah again:

> But if I say, 'I will not mention him or speak any more in his name,' his word is in my heart like a fire, a fire shut up in my bones. I am weary of holding it in; indeed, I cannot. (Jeremiah 20:9)

He's God's spokesperson, but wherever he goes he is ridiculed for his faith: despite that he keeps on serving God because he can't hold the fire of God inside him – he has to let it out! Then things happen:

> 'I have heard what the prophets say who prophesy lies in my name. They say, "I had a dream! I had a dream!" How long will this continue in the hearts of these lying prophets, who prophesy the delusions of their own minds? They think the dreams they tell one another will make my people forget my name, just as their fathers forgot my name through Baal worship. Let the prophet who has a dream tell his dream, but let the one who has my word speak it faithfully. For what has straw to do with grain?' declares the LORD. 'Is not my word like fire,' declares the LORD, 'and like a hammer that breaks a rock in pieces?' (Jeremiah 23:25–29)

But perhaps the most important imagery of fire in the Bible are the following two passages. First when God appears to Moses:

> There the angel of the LORD appeared to him in flames of fire from within a bush. Moses saw that though the bush was on fire it did not burn up. (Exodus 3:2)

If you read the rest of Exodus chapter 3 you will see that this is where God reveals His uniqueness, His holiness, and His compassion for His creation.

Second, when the Holy Spirit arrives at Pentecost:

> They saw what seemed to be tongues of fire that separated and came to rest on each of them. All of them were filled with the Holy Spirit and began to speak in other tongues as the Spirit enabled them. (Acts 2:3–4)

So fire is intimately linked with God giving us a new and powerful revelation of Himself.

IGNITE is firstly, but not exclusively, aimed at 'church kids' like I was. The aim of IGNITE isn't to create a cosy Christian subculture but rather to grow a counterculture that is strong in Jesus and constantly looking to bring Jesus into the lives of individuals and into situations. IGNITE is also ideal for new Christians to set down their standard for Christian living. Looking back on my own life, I realise there was a long gap between becoming a Christian and then really taking seriously a life of discipleship. IGNITE can help immensely in shortening that gap in your life!

In this book you'll find a combination of illustrations from life and teaching from the Bible. Each chapter includes a different email message sent to the IGNITE website from a variety of young people. God is at work in the lives of this generation! There is also a 'real-life' story from a young person involved with IGNITE in each chapter, along with the specific IGNITE declaration point that the chapter is unpacking. I'd encourage you to take the 'Firestarters' seriously – a few practical pointers at the end of each chapter to help you keep the flame burning.

Don't get fooled into thinking, however, that simply using the IGNITE declaration or the Firestarters as a tick list will solve all your problems! God is more passionate about your heart (how you feel and what your motives are) than about the things you sign up for or even do. So the important thing about IGNITE and this book is your heart response to it. Don't even bother to sign up to IGNITE or put the Firestarters into practice unless your heart is really in it.

In the book of Joel we read this command from God: 'Rend your heart and not your garments' (Joel 2:13). In other words, God was fed up with the religious leaders making a great public gesture of ripping their clothes in two as a sign of their repentance and commitment without really meaning it deep down. He was looking for a heart gesture and He still is. You can probably identify, even from your own life, instances where people have supposedly committed to something but haven't been able to back it up. So the public lifestyle that IGNITE commends to you can only be an out-working of the love and passion you have for God that overflows from your heart.

My prayer is simply that this book will help equip you for the exciting journey of faith that God has in store for you. It's a foundation to help you build for the future. So get excited, get fired up, get passionate, unquench-able, consumed, in short – IGNITE!

THREE SIMPLE WORDS

Starting the Christian journey is absolutely essential, and if you have never done that or aren't sure how to start the journey, then follow these three simple words. To go on this journey of faith, your relationship with God must be right. If you know you have never put your faith and trust in God before, then carefully read, take to heart and act upon the following.

Becoming a Christian is all about change – change of mind; change of direction; change of lifestyle. That's what conversion is! Going God's way from now on and not your own. God's the centre of your world now, not you!

SORRY You have to ask God to forgive you for being self-centred and for all the bad things in your life that have come from focusing on yourself and not God. Unless you say sorry and turn away from your selfishness you will be separated from God for ever. 'Anyone united with the Messiah gets a fresh start, is

created new. The old life is gone; a new life burgeons!'
(2 Corinthians 5:7, *The Message*)

*PRAY – Sorry, God, for going my own way instead of your
way. I want to say sorry for all the bad stuff in my life. I will
change from my way to your way.* 'If we confess our sins,
he is faithful and just and will forgive us our sins and
purify us from all unrighteousness.' (1 John 1:9)

THANKS You need to thank Jesus for dying on the
cross for you and for His offer of forgiveness, freedom
and new life. The death of Jesus means He loves you
immensely, has taken the punishment that you really
deserve for your selfishness. It means God wipes the
slate clean of all the bad stuff in your life, and you're
free to start a new life as part of God's family.

*PRAY – Thank you Jesus for dying on the cross and taking the
punishment I deserve. Thank you for your love and your
forgiveness. This means I can be free to be part of your family.*
'For God so loved the world that he gave his one and
only Son, that whoever believes in him shall not perish
but have eternal life.' (John 3:16)

PLEASE You need to accept God's offer and invite him
to come and live in your life by His Spirit. The same
power that brought Jesus back to life is available for
you to become the person God wants you to be. He

wants to be in charge of your life and change you even more day by day. As you promise to turn away from evil and live for Christ, the Holy Spirit can give you the strength to keep this promise.

PRAY – Please come into my life now by your Holy Spirit and change my life. Please help me clear out all the bad stuff. Please take charge of all I do and help me live as one of your followers for ever. In Jesus' name, Amen.

2

the ride of your life

In the autumn of 1998 I was invited to be part of a nationwide tour of the United States with my friends, the band 'Newsboys'. I'd known the guys for several years and had worked with them in Europe a few times, but this was to be the first time I'd travelled on tour with them in America. My role was to speak to the concert audience each night and challenge them to go on a short-term mission trip with the ministry 'Teen Mania' in the following summer.

I can remember standing nervously beside the stage at a theme park in Charlotte, North Carolina; it was my first night on tour and I was just about to go on and speak. I had spent two days learning all the right cues for the video technician to bring in various pieces of video footage, only to be told ten minutes beforehand that, because it was open air, we couldn't use the video that night!

Seven thousand people were showing their appreciation for the support band 'Third Day' when a guy who I thought was their guitar technician came up to me and said, 'Are you the speaker tonight?' He then proceeded to calm me down with a great prayer. I walked on stage thinking 'Wow! These American bands are incredible – even their roadies are awesome men of God.' When I came off stage 20 minutes later, I found out that the guy who had prayed for me was Third Day's travelling pastor, John Poitevent, from Atlanta. John became a really close friend, but that night he did something that I will never forget – and I'm not sure I'll ever forgive him for it, either. He persuaded me to go on the Top Gun ride in the theme park with all the members of Third Day, with the words, 'It'll be the ride of your life.'

'No big deal' you are saying to yourself, but you have to realise that I have a built-in fear of theme park rides – I am the man who went on the Alice-in-Wonderland teacup ride at Disney with my daughter who was four at the time, while my wife and son went on the Tower of Terror!

Anyway, I succumbed to the peer group pressure of six newly-found friends and struggled manfully on to the Top Gun ride – rated by US navy pilots as frighteningly realistic.

It must have been among the worst experiences of my life, not helped by the fact that all the way around cameras were taking pictures of us. At the end of the ride we were offered these photos to buy, but I didn't really have a need for pictures that showed me with my head buried in my chest and my eyes screwed tightly shut! It definitely was not the ride of my life! About on a par with riding the rapids on the Zambezi river – another big mistake I made!

If there is one thing that I have discovered about rides and life it is this: the biggest and best, most complete, most incredible, awesome and challenging ride you will ever go on is the journey you undertake following Jesus with no holds barred. It's the journey you were made for and it's the journey that makes sense of your world. It's the journey that you have to grab with everything you have got; it's the journey that ignites a passion for Jesus; it's the journey that millions of people have travelled on in the last 2,000 years and it's the journey that is the starting premise for the IGNITE initiative and for this book.

Join me on this journey right now.

To help you get fired up here are three guidelines for you to take with you.

1. Make the most of the moment

Have you ever missed out on the opportunity to do something and then bitterly regretted it later? A year or so after I'd met John Poitevent, the guy who prayed for me on the first night of the Newsboys tour, he was coming to stay with me at home in Cardiff. That night at the St David's Hall in Cardiff, the famous American singer-songwriter James Taylor was playing. I thought about getting tickets but decided against it because John would be tired from his flight and train journey, and being a bit younger than me he might not appreciate James Taylor. So we were sitting down having a cup of coffee when I casually mentioned that we could have gone to see James Taylor. John was distraught. 'You're joking!' he said, 'You mean you didn't get tickets for James Taylor? He's a legend!'

I felt pretty stupid, but the story doesn't end there. Three months later John and I were in his home city of Atlanta, Georgia, and we had a spare night. We went out to eat, saw a film, and ended up about midnight in a coffee shop. A crowd of girls excitedly arrived at the next table, looking like they'd had a great evening. When the waitress asked them what they'd been up to you can imagine the sick looks on the faces of John and I when we heard they'd been to see James Taylor in the Atlanta Symphony Hall. We'd managed to miss James Taylor twice, once on each side of the Atlantic, in the space of three months! You feel pretty bad when you miss out!

I want to challenge you not to miss out on what God has in store for you. In the first chapter of Mark's Gospel, we read this:

> 'The time has come,' he said. 'The kingdom of God is near. Repent and believe the good news!' As Jesus walked beside the Sea of Galilee, he saw Simon and his brother Andrew casting a net into the lake, for they were fishermen. 'Come, follow me,' Jesus said, 'and I will make you fishers of men.' At once they left their nets and followed him. (Mark 1:15–18)

This is the start of the disciples' journey with Jesus, and reminds us that one of the basic principles about being a Christian is actually following Christ. Here Jesus is talking about decision time. He's saying it's here now – the time not just to repent of your sins and your selfishness, but the time also to let God change you radically and adopt a completely new lifestyle. God doesn't want you just to be a believer; He wants you to be a disciple, and there is no place for half-heartedness. Once you have met Jesus, life can no longer be the same. It's as if two new signs are put up in a shop window. One says UNDER NEW MANAGEMENT and the other says NO MORE BUSINESS AS USUAL. In other words, Jesus rules your life now and things are going to change.

2. God wants to consume you

When I first heard the band Third Day I was belatedly introduced to one of their big hits: the song called 'Consuming Fire'. I heard it every night for two months, just before I was due to speak, and it challenged me to really take seriously the verses in the Bible that talk about God in these terms. In Paul's letter to the Hebrews he refers to God as a consuming fire, a phrase first used in Deuteronomy: 'For the LORD your God is a consuming fire, a jealous God' (Deuteronomy 4:24).

When I read this scripture afresh it shook me that God could be described as 'jealous' – surely that was a negative emotion, a selfish thing to be. But here's the deal – God wants all of your life, every part of it. You've probably heard it said that 'either He's Lord of all or He's not Lord at all'. You see, you can't give a bit of your life to God – you have to let Him have it all.

Too many of us have said to God, 'OK, You can have my Sundays and one night a week, and some of my money and part of my holiday time and 20 minutes of my thoughts each day,' but the rest we have kept for ourselves. Yet God loves us so much and regards each of us as so special that He wants to be involved in absolutely every part of our lives.

That can be good news and bad news. It's good news to think that all the struggles and worries we have, all the parts of our life we can't cope with alone, God wants to be Lord of. It's bad news for us if there are parts of our life that we have selfishly kept away from God.

More accurately, the context of the verse in Deuteronomy is a warning about having other idols before God, and this is where God gets jealous. He wants you to have nothing in your life that is more important than Him – not your family or your job or your future or anything. In this context, God's jealousy is a very positive dimension to His character; He demands such a total life response from us that just one part not given over, just one thing made more important, brings forth His jealousy.

Just think about God being a consuming fire for a moment. Fire burns stuff up; it's used to get rid of the rubbish and it helps to clean as it does so. Precious metals are refined as they are heated to high temperatures, and whatever impurities are present rise to the top of the molten metal and can be skimmed off, leaving the pure stuff behind. God wants to consume you like that every day. He wants to heat you up with His fire so that you become purer and purer and so that more and more of your life comes under his Lordship.

Fire also provides a source of power, and when you are consumed by God's fire then the same power that raised Jesus from the dead is available to you today.

Which would you rather be? A half-hearted pew-warmer stuck in a set of boring rules and regulations?

Or a follower of Jesus, who has the passion and fire of God consuming you and igniting you into action? The choice is yours!

✉ **FROM THE WEB** ✉

'I reckon two of the biggest issues amongst teen Christians are lukewarmness and lack of purity. Hey, I'm supposed to have left teendom behind and I still can't get it sorted! The patterns you put in place for yourself now will probably stick with you for most of your life. So let's get serious with God and get ourselves sorted, in His strength and grace. Let's take Him at His word and show true obedience. We can't preach it if we don't live it, guys, and I don't know about you but I want to see revival in my time. So let's get going.'

3. God wants to use you

Steve Redgrave, the five-times Olympic gold medal-winning rower, tells the story of when he was selected in 1978 to row for the British junior team for the first time in the world championships. He was a year younger than the other boys selected, and when two of the boys in the four heard that an unknown, untried, inexperienced rower younger than them had been selected, they withdrew from the boat saying they didn't want to row with a no-hoper!

Redgrave goes on to say that somewhere now there

must be two men aged 40 or so kicking themselves at being so stupid!

I believe with all my heart that God never looks down on you in the same judgemental way that those two boys viewed Steve Redgrave. Never does God say you are too young or too inexperienced or that you are a nobody with no hope. In fact, God says exactly the opposite. You might have made the same mistake about God that I used to make – thinking that you had to be good enough for God to use you. Then I learnt a crucial lesson that is littered throughout the Bible. The qualification to be used by God isn't ability; it's availability. What matters is being *willing* to be used by God – that's always more important than how talented you might be.

In my last year of university I started off the football season playing in the fifth team, but by the end of the season I was playing in the second team! Had my game dramatically improved over a number of months? Was I getting friendly with the selection committee? No on both counts. All that happened was that as more and more players lost interest in playing I remained available all season, and in the final few weeks we only had a first and second team because that's all the players we had available. I was selected not on ability but on availability. Get the picture? That's how God's team operates too.

When we read the Bible I think that sometimes we believe that all the great biblical heroes were old men with long white beards who lived to be over 100. While that is sometimes the case we miss the fact that many young people were called by God too.

When Joseph's dreams from God started in Genesis 37, he was a young man of 17. David was the youngest of Jesse's sons and was herding sheep when he fought Goliath. Josiah was eight years of age when he became king and 'did what was right in the eyes of the Lord' (you can read his story in 2 Kings 22). Jeremiah wasn't sure he was old enough or eloquent enough to serve God:

> 'Ah, Sovereign LORD,' I said, 'I do not know how to speak; I am only a child.' But the LORD said to me, 'Do not say, "I am only a child." You must go to everyone I send you to and say whatever I command you. Do not be afraid of them, for I am with you and will rescue you,' declares the LORD. (Jeremiah 1:6–8)

In the New Testament we see Mary the mother of Jesus being visited by an angel when she was a young teenager, and replying, 'I am the Lord's servant.' John Mark and Timothy were certainly both young when they started travelling with Paul on his missionary journeys. Or how about the boy who handed his lunch over for Jesus to do something miraculous with?

Young people aren't exempt from the call of God; in fact they are often in the front line of His recruits. When Jesus sent the 72 followers out in pairs he told them this:

'The harvest is plentiful, but the workers are few. Ask the Lord of the harvest, therefore, to send out workers into his harvest field. Go! I am sending you out like lambs among wolves. (Luke 10:2–3)

The harvest is still plentiful, there is still so much Kingdom work to be done, and Jesus still wants to send 'lambs' out on his behalf. Are you ready for it? Don't wait until you are older or more experienced; don't let other priorities creep in. God wants you now!

Where these three things come together – the cross

There is one place where God's desire is for you not to accept business as usual, where He claims all of you, and where it becomes possible for you to be used by God. That place is the cross of Jesus; the place where God's love and righteousness meet, where His compassion and justice are joined.

While I've been writing this book Big Ideas had a mission team of young people from Cardiff travelling to Amsterdam for an Easter outreach. BBC Radio Wales asked if the team could take a tape recorder with them to compile an audio diary of the trip. When the BBC guy came into our office with the tape recorder and micro-phone it was immediately seized from him by Pete, who works with us in Big Ideas. Pete began to play at being a news reporter and started recording his own voice.

Noticing that Pete hadn't set any levels and was speaking too loudly, the man from the BBC said, 'That'll be horribly distorted and completely unusable.' Rather wickedly, I replied that he'd just described Pete's whole life.

Being completely serious though, the BBC guy had effectively summed up the state of the human condition. My life and your life are horribly distorted and completely unusable without the cross of Jesus. The world we live in is horribly distorted and completely unusable without the cross of Jesus. It's on the cross that God punishes the horrible distortions in our life, and Jesus takes that punishment. It's on the cross that God takes hold of lives ruined by sin and selfishness and turns them into lives that can be used for His glory. It's because of the cross that our response to Jesus must be to be totally consumed. When we see his ultimate sacrifice for us, we want to give our all to Him and allow Him to use us however He decides.

When Jesus was crucified there were two thieves executed, one either side of Him. It's revealing to see the different responses to Jesus of these two common criminals. One is very cynical of Jesus, but the other one recognises Jesus for who He is and the immense power of forgiveness He has.

Even with his dying breath on a cross, that thief receives eternal life from God. However distorted you think your life may be, whatever horrible memories you have, whether self-inflicted or from others, however worthless and beyond use you think you are, the cross incredibly, completely and permanently changes all of that.

Can you really turn around from your past? Can you really let God consume every part of you? Can you really be used to serve God? Jesus' death on the cross says you can. If you trust in the cross you will never be completely unusable to God, and you will want to discover His purpose for your life and develop a passionate desire to follow Jesus with everything you have got.

The IGNITE declaration is simply about living a life that backs up your passion for Jesus and your desire to change, to be consumed by God and to be used to advance His kingdom.

REAL-LIFE STORY

Naomi Hill is 23 and is the National Youth Evangelist for The Evangelisation Society in partnership with Big Ideas.

'I became a Christian at the age of eleven. I'd asked my parents if I could go to Sunday school when I was four. No one in my family went to church, and I don't really know why I asked to go to church – but looking back I can see God was obviously at work. I believed everything I was taught at church and that process came to a climax when someone said that I

could become a Christian there and then.

'I knew the people in church had something I needed and I wanted to be like them too. I continued to be part of the youth group and the church but didn't really do the 'being a Christian at school' thing very well.

'To be honest, it was a massive struggle to live my life as a Christian. Then along came the Cardiff Alive Mission in September of 1995. I can clearly remember attending a massive event at the Cardiff International Arena, and that night God spoke to me. As clear as anything He said to me, "It's not your life to live; it's my life to live through you." I began to realise what it meant to be crucified with Christ like Paul talks about in Galatians 2:20, and I knew I needed to be dead to myself but alive in Jesus. God showed me the reasons why I was on this earth: one was to know God and experience life with Him, and the other was to play my part in helping others know God and experience life with Him. I went home from the Cardiff International Arena and wrote down everything God had revealed to me.

'An immediate effect of this was that I gave up some of my own plans. I'd been keen to travel around Europe after my A levels with my friend Ruth, but the day after the Cardiff Alive event I felt I had to go into school and tell Ruth I couldn't go with her. It wasn't my life to do with what I wanted any more – it was God's.

'Quite soon after this a church leader talked to me about Bible college and so off I went for three years. It was as simple as that! There was nothing else I wanted to do: I didn't want to spend three years on anything else, and I definitely didn't want to waste it. Bible college was obviously and definitely the place for me. At college I met Christians from different churches and different countries and began to see that God's plan was so much bigger than just me. It was at college that God began to teach me how I could serve Him more effectively. I discovered the areas of ministry I was passionate about and the areas that weren't really for me, too.

'From college it was a natural progression to begin work as an evangelist with Big Ideas. God had it all planned out in fact. I didn't really know the Big Ideas guys very well but they were looking for a college graduate, and a mutual friend made the link between them and me. I knew I was called to evangelism – I'm a young person, and I love sharing Jesus with other young people.

'It's been an amazing opportunity to be based in my home city and travel around sharing the gospel. I'm really excited about IGNITE, because it's not just about telling people the good news, it's about getting them to live out the good news all the time. I know how tough that can be, especially if you are the only Christian in your family, for example. It's easy to go to church or a Christian gathering but then come home and feel like you are left with nothing. So the encouragement and commitment that the IGNITE declaration brings is vital.

'In my Christian life I have always based things on a personal decision; I've never relied on anyone else's beliefs. Sometimes it has been hard to make those personal decisions. At school, for example, not to smoke and drink when almost *everyone else does. IGNITE definitely helps young people make lifestyle decisions for themselves, with God's guidance, and enables them to stand up and be different.*

'Evangelism could be my middle name really; it's my passion and the thing that keeps my life going. I believe that God has placed me in my family, and I'm learning all the time how to live out my life for Christ with them. I'm passionate about living for Jesus and I'm passionate about my family too.

'I always look back to God's specific call on my life, in the Cardiff International Arena, and trust that call – even if other circumstances or opportunities in my life change. At the same time, though, I'm willing to hear from God about new challenges he wants to put my way. I take great inspiration from the parable of the persistent widow in Luke 18. It gives me a reminder to keep praying for things I really want to happen.

'Friends at college will remember me as a tiny, quiet girl and now I'm an evangelist working with TES and Big Ideas. It's so exciting! I believe very simply that all I've done is to make myself available to God and discover his purpose for my life. He has honoured the fact that I've laid down my life for Him, and the life I now live with Him is so much better than the one I'd be leading on my own. I love Jesus!'

IGNITE DECLARATION

I believe that God has a special purpose for my generation and me. I ask God to IGNITE in me a desire to discover this purpose.

FIRESTARTERS

- Make a commitment before God that your life will no longer be 'business as usual'.
- Offer all of your life to God so that He can consume you.
- Make yourself willing and available to God to be used in whichever way He desires.

3

don't wanna be like
elvis presley

I used to do lots of missions and youth events with a band called 'Fresh Claim'. They were fronted by a man called Simon Law, who is now an Anglican vicar. One of their favourite songs was called 'Don't wanna be like' which talked about the stupidity of trying to model ourselves on any of the so-called superstars in the world.

The first verse simply stated 'Don't wanna be like Elvis Presley'. Whenever Fresh Claim used to sing this song I would then do a talk featuring some interesting statistics. Research has shown that when Elvis died there were 34 people who earned their living as Elvis impersonators. This figure had jumped to 8,000 or so by the early 1990s, and by the year 2037, 1 in 5 people living would be an Elvis impersonator! You can prove anything by statistics, but Elvis is probably the most impersonated man in history; my next-door neighbours even travelled to Las Vegas to renew their wedding vows with an Elvis impersonator in attendance.

Of course, the point is; why bother to impersonate anyone like Elvis when the Bible calls us to be imitators of Jesus? These next two chapters tackle this very issue.

The cross of Jesus makes a demand on those of us who follow Him. It should be like a brand mark on our lives. Rather than living for Nike or Calvin Klein or Hugo Boss or any of the other myriad of designer labels, our lives should bear the design of God and the mark of Jesus so that people can see who we belong to. For myself, however, I have to admit that there have been times when although I've been a Christian I've lived like a 'practical atheist'. Do you know what I mean? Someone who believes it all in their head but has real trouble putting it into practice! Recognise yourself at all?

In Mark 10 the rich young ruler comes up to Jesus and asks a great question: 'What must I do to inherit eternal life?' The trouble was he believed that if he only kept a rule or two that would be good enough. He'd been doing all the spiritually correct stuff but it still wasn't right. The problem wasn't the stuff he was doing but the state of his heart. He hadn't realised that rules and regulations weren't the most important things for Jesus but that relationship was the key. Sadly, the young man had something in his life that was more important to him than a relationship with Jesus, and until he changed that priority then whatever else he did just wouldn't matter.

It's not enough to go to church, read the books, listen to the music and be part of the crowd – you must open up every area of your existence to Jesus. In Galatians 6 Paul says that his body bears the marks of Jesus. He was possibly talking about the marks left by various beatings and stonings he had suffered for his faith. The word he chooses to use that we translate as 'marks' is a word that would have been associated with the branding mark on a slave or an animal to signify ownership. I want to suggest to you that there are four key areas where you need the marks of Jesus in your life.

✉ **FROM THE WEB** ✉

'As I was walking into uni today some stuff came flooding into my mind. As Christians we are supposed to say "I no longer live but Christ lives in me" and "my life is not my own" and "I have been crucified in the flesh". How many of us can say those sincerely? If it's true, then how come we do stuff that we know for sure Jesus would never do?'

1. Your thoughts

If there is one area in which I have constantly struggled over the years it is in my thought life. Jesus made it clear that merely playing out a sinful action in our heart and mind was as bad as actually committing it in reality. If that's the case then my score on the Ten Commandments is nought out of ten. I'm not too despondent, though, and neither should you be if you are in the same boat. Even the apostle Paul knew of the battle raging in his mind and knew that it could only be won with God's help.

> So I find this law at work: When I want to do good, evil is right there with me. For in my inner being I delight in God's law; but I see another law at work in the members of my body, waging war against the law of my mind and making me a prisoner of the law of sin at work within my members. What a wretched man I am! Who will rescue me from this body of death? Thanks be to God — through Jesus Christ our Lord! (Romans 7:21–25)

We live in a world that constantly invades our mind with attitudes and thoughts that are completely contrary to Christian living. I'm definitely not a person who believes that everything in the world is evil; in fact I like to embrace contemporary culture and enjoy an evening watching TV or going to the cinema or a concert. But I do believe that we are being barraged by a mind-set and a world-view that goes against the gospel and can so easily dominate our own thinking.

Paul's strategy for winning the battle in our mind is as follows:

Do not conform any longer to the pattern of this world, but be transformed by the renewing of your mind. Then you will be able to test and approve what God's will is — his good, pleasing and perfect will. (Romans 12:2)

In other words, we have to ask Jesus to be present in our thoughts, our outlooks, our understanding and our perceptions and for Him to constantly clear our minds of any rubbish that may have gathered there. It's only then that we'll be able to understand God's will in our lives. We'll look at that more in detail in the final chapter of this book.

Key words here are *truth* and *discipline*. If you aren't really sure what you believe and why you believe it then you need to soak your thoughts in truth and you'll find that truth in Scripture. Ask yourself the question, 'What is God's truth for my life and the world around me?' When the world is screaming at you in so many different ways, you need to be certain of the truth. This is where discipline comes in. Learn to discipline yourself against sinful thoughts and selfish thinking. There will be times when you have to switch the TV off, stop a conversation, close a magazine, and actively seek God in order to win the battle of your mind. Allow Jesus to be included in your thought life and ask the Holy Spirit to protect you from deception. Let the truths that God wants to teach you through the IGNITE declaration sink deep into your heart and mind.

2. Your relationships

When Jesus impacts your thinking, that immediately has a knock-on effect on your daily living, and no more strongly so than in your relationships. In my weaker moments I sometimes think how much easier life would be without other people! Yet God has placed us in relationship – first with Himself and then with the people around us. I meet so many Christians who are living in a state of turmoil because they have got messed-up relationships. Like so many of the issues I'm addressing in this book, relationships deserve a whole book on their own, but I'm going to touch on three main areas. I believe you need to include Jesus in your relationships with your family, with the opposite sex and with your friends who aren't Christians.

Now I expect some of you are reading this and saying, 'If only you knew my situation, you'd realise how difficult it is being a Christian in my family, with my friends, with my boyfriend or girlfriend, husband or wife.' I know how difficult relationships can be! My family upbringing was a challenging one, with my natural father deserting us when I was seven. We've experienced the heartbreak of divorce and various other family upheavals along the way. Similarly I've known the agony of getting relationships with the opposite sex completely wrong because I didn't put Jesus first. I've also missed opportunities to build strong evangelistic and discipling relationships with friends who weren't Christians, because my priorities were wrong.

I can't give you a short-cut to success in relationships because it's not as simple as that. But THE big step is to include Jesus – let Him be part of every relationship that you have, pour your heart out to Him about your relationships and allow Him to get your thinking straight about each one. Let's face it, we'll all make a better job of our relationships when we surrender them to Jesus. The next chapter will give you some practical guidance for growing closer to Jesus, and you might want to use that as an opportunity to include Him in your relationships. Happy or sad, family or friends, Christians or not, romantic or platonic, spoiled or strong, public or private – whatever the state of your relationships, hand them over to Jesus now.

3. Your resources

Towards the end of the first book of Chronicles, King David is about to hand over the throne to his son Solomon. Solomon's great vision is to rebuild the Temple, and as they are gathering gifts to help with the building David says this to God in the presence of the people:

> Yours, O LORD, is the greatness and the power and the glory and the majesty and the splendour, for everything in

heaven and earth is yours. Yours, O LORD, is the kingdom; you are exalted as head over all. Wealth and honour come from you; you are the ruler of all things. In your hands are strength and power to exalt and give strength to all. Now, our God, we give you thanks, and praise your glorious name. But who am I, and who are my people, that we should be able to give as generously as this? Everything comes from you, and we have given you only what comes from your hand. (1 Chronicles 29:11–14)

When we adopt the same attitude as David we won't go far wrong in handling our resources, because when we realise that everything we have comes from God in the first place it makes it so much easier to include Jesus in all that we do with what we have! I want to challenge you to look carefully at three areas of resource that God has given you.

The first one is *time*. When you take out time spent sleeping, eating, growing as a small child, and sickness, there isn't as much time left in a normal lifetime as you thought you had. So what do you spend most of your time on, and do you include Jesus in all the time that you have?

When you take out time spent watching TV, surfing the Internet, playing computer games, listening to music, it's easy to see how sometimes Jesus gets squeezed into only a tiny proportion of your day. We've already established that God wants to be Lord of every part of our lives so He should be Lord of however we spend our time. Yet, more than that, if you are serious about following Jesus and developing an intimate friendship with Him, then that will take a sacrifice of time to pray, to read your Bible, to meet with other Christians and to serve God in whatever way He demands.

The second one is *talents*. All of you who read this book will have some talent or other that God has given to you. You may still be in a process of trying to discover what that talent is, but believe me – it is there! Are you prepared to include Jesus in that talent and use it to glorify God, or would you rather use it for selfish means? I'd always been a bit puzzled by the parable of the talents in Matthew 25. Then, as I read it again one day, I began to understand it. If you read it you might think, like me, that the issue is about how many talents each servant is given. It's not! It's all about what they do with what they have got. I am a man of one or two small talents (just ask the people I work with!) but I really delight in putting them to use for the kingdom. I can't imagine any greater feeling than to know that God has taken hold of an ability or gift that I have and then used it for His glory.

The third one is *money*. When God comes into your life He also comes into your wallet. Are you including Jesus in all that you do with your finances? The simple fact is that whether you are rich or poor, whether you have plenty of disposable income or your wallet is permanently empty, Jesus wants to be Lord of your finances. Deep down you'll already know how much of a massive impact your money could make to gospel ministry in many parts of the world. A very practical way to begin including Jesus in your money is to commit to financially supporting your church or another Christian ministry with small monthly amounts.

Here at Big Ideas we wouldn't have survived the first few years of our existence as a charity without a core group of people who stood by us financially month by month, regularly giving small but vital amounts. Each of us working in Big Ideas also individually supports other ministries: for example, all of us are involved in a child sponsorship programme, which means that a regular amount from us brings food, clothing, education and Jesus into the lives of a child somewhere overseas. Listening to a friend talk recently, he described sponsoring a child as 'baseline' Christianity – in other words, the very least and most basic commitment we should be making with our money.

4. Your future

I love the story in Luke 12 of the farming man who has a few good crops and decides to store them up and live happily ever after. He thinks that the rest of his life can consist of eating, drinking, enjoying himself and taking it easy. In most translations this passage is titled 'the rich fool' because no sooner has he made these plans for a comfortable future than he finds out he's going to lose his life that night!

Don't plan for the future yourself – include Jesus in it. God has something special in store for you and you'll discover more about that in the final chapter of this book, but right now commit to trusting God for your future. Lay down all your plans and ambitions, for career, family, education, travel, house, reputation, whatever they may be, and allow your future to be inspired and motivated by God.

> Now listen, you who say, 'Today or tomorrow we will go to this or that city, spend a year there, carry on business and make money.' Why, you do not even know what will happen tomorrow. What is your life? You are a mist that appears for a little while and then vanishes. Instead, you ought to say, 'If it is the Lord's will, we will live and do this or that.' As it is, you boast and brag. All such boasting is evil. (James 4:13–16)

The marks of Jesus must be clearly visible in our lives. They are the evidence of our walk with Jesus and our commitment to Him. Jesus wants to brand us outside and inside with His marks. That's what the Lordship of Jesus is all about. When doubting Thomas meets the disciples who have seen the risen Jesus, he says: 'Unless I see the nail marks in his hands and put my finger where the nails were, and put my hand into his side,

I will not believe it' (John 20:25).

When he actually sees these marks it is a different story: 'Thomas said to him, "My Lord and my God!"' (verse 28).

When people see the marks of Jesus on our life, they may experience the same change as Thomas.

REAL-LIFE STORY

Matt Gregor is a 21-year-old student who has been a volunteer with Big Ideas for six years.

'Regularly going to church, listening to sermons and being surrounded by Christian family and friends who invested in me, all helped include Jesus in my life. I can remember going along to missions and crusades from an early age, and I particularly remember responding to the gospel at a Luis Palau meeting in 1989 when I was just nine years old. Even at that age I knew I was making a conscious decision to live for Jesus, to serve Him, and to read the Bible as much as I could. A big, big help was having plenty of people interested in me and my walk with God.

'Like most young people, I initially found that including Jesus in my school life was a bit of a struggle. It wasn't until my last couple of years at secondary school that I got a focus on the situation and decided that the best thing to do was to live my life at school for Jesus and think, 'Who cares what anybody else thinks?' I wanted to stand up for who I believed

in, not just by saying I went to church at the weekend and count that as witnessing, but actually living like, and talking about, the Lord Jesus.

'I wanted to let my school friends know about Jesus in real terms. Being involved in the Christian Union at school isn't always the most popular thing to do, but in my last 18 months there I did get stuck into it and tried to raise its profile. There's no doubt that through some of the stuff we did, people heard the good news of Jesus. I took a significant step of faith in organising a trip from my school in Caerphilly to Alton Towers theme park, where the World Wide Message Tribe were in concert. We ended up with two coaches and over 100 people coming along. Over 70 of them weren't Christians, and as well as having a great day on the rides and amusements they saw the concert and heard Jesus being talked about in a relevant way.

'I was only 17 when I arranged this and got criticism from all sorts of angles – some people thought the cost was too much, others said I should be concentrating on my school work and some teachers were concerned that it wasn't an official school trip. I knew that we were going to go for it and maintained a determination that people would hear the gospel and come closer to accepting Jesus into their lives. It helped having about 30 Christians on the trip, and we'd been praying for it in preparation. Simply speaking, I knew this trip was to glorify Jesus and so I tried to act with integrity throughout all the planning and on the day itself.

'For many of my contemporaries at school, the thought of

going to university was seen as a licence to party. I made the decision from the word go that I would include Jesus completely and consciously in my university life. In fact I wanted my life to be a shining light for Him and I wanted to show Jesus to people through every aspect of my life.

'I started off at Glamorgan University by living at home, but quickly decided I could be a more effective witness in halls of residence, so moved in. The accountability of my local church and of the university Christian Union really helped me stay strong and focused on Jesus and meant I could keep Him at the centre of my life. In my second year I became President of the Christian Union and saw this as a further opportunity to serve God. The leadership was something I took seriously and wanted to bring a fresh approach to. It was also something that I totally laid before Jesus – it was His strength through the Holy Spirit that would drive me on, rather than any selfish motive or personal talent.

'The CU leadership was very time-consuming but I had already developed a sacrificial attitude with my time. For a number of years, when friends were off on exotic summer holidays I was on mission, summer camps or other outreach teams and had always found real spiritual growth from committing time to serve God. At university, though, I wanted to balance time between the CU, my studies, my friends in Hall and on my course. Trusting God throughout was always the best thing to do. I've consistently tried to include Jesus in my thoughts and my conversation, not just thinking about Him or talking about Him, but by having thoughts and conversations that honour Him. What we think and what we say to a certain extent come from what we read, watch or listen to because what we take in we give out. So I try to keep taking good stuff in, believing what the Bible says in Philippians: 'If anything is excellent or praiseworthy – think about such things.'

'When I'm driving I try to listen to Christian music or teaching tapes rather than automatically turning the radio on, and to be honest, for the last two or three years I really haven't watched much TV. I know that there is a battle going on in my mind and I want Jesus to be Lord of my thoughts. I have to say to myself sometimes, "I am not going to think about that; I'm going to think about the things of the Lord." Every battle that Jesus helps me win makes it easier to face the next one. Talking and sharing with Christian friends is a big help too: cultivating conversations that are kind, encouraging and pure means that these things rub off in the rest of my life.

'Relationships with the opposite sex are always likely to be an area of temptation for people my age, so, just as in every other area of life, I try to include Jesus. Practically, that means going for a pure life and keeping the relationship out in the open, with nothing being behind closed doors. I try to lead a pure life and have a clear conscience before Jesus. I have found that what really helps my relationships with others is to spend time praying about the people I have friendships with. By bringing them before God in prayer I gain the strength to make sure the friendship develops in a godly direction.

'I always want to include Jesus in every decision I make

because they all affect my character. I'm so encouraged by IGNITE because it helps young people to focus on godly living and making decisions that glorify Jesus. The fact that Jesus is my Lord means that I don't live to please myself but I live to please Him. I want my attitudes, my words and my actions to be pleasing to God. By including Jesus, it actually benefits my life incredibly because there is no better direction for me to go than to follow Him.

'I was recently a source of amusement at work when I went shopping at lunchtime to buy a ream of paper rather than helping myself to stationery in the office. I knew that would be wrong and that God has better things in store for me, but some colleagues thought I was very strange.

'I genuinely see myself as a missionary where I am in industry and always want to do an honest day's work and treat people with dignity and respect. Working closely with a group of people means you get to know them well, and there are times when I have had to ask Jesus for patience, calmness and restraint in my language – not just with my work colleagues but also with customers who are angry about work not completed satisfactorily. On a number of instances when I have made mistakes personally I've owned up rather than look to blame someone else. I really need to focus on Jesus when it's tough to be kind and gracious against the odds.

'Some of my favourite Bible characters are from the Old Testament and include Joseph, who was a dreamer: I can associate with him because I long to see God move in power across our country as he has done in the past. Even when his brothers left him for dead in a hole, Joseph was determined to stay focused on God.

'David is another of my favourites: he was a worshipper and a man after God's own heart. I want to be like him, worshipping God in all that I do and say, and living a life that is pleasing to Him. Living a godly life in the secret place, is as important as in the public places. So I make efforts to keep Jesus with me all the time – especially when I don't have any people around.

'Taking the time to be at church regularly and to attend more than just the Sunday morning service helps me include Jesus in my life. Neither David nor Joseph were perfect people (they both made mistakes) and I can certainly relate to that. For both of them, God provided a fresh start, and to any of you reading this who might feel a failure at the moment, I would encourage you to make a fresh start. It's no good relying on yesterday – you have to include Jesus fresh each day. God's grace and mercy is new to us each day. God's heart is one of kindness and compassion and He wants good things for us. We can't depend upon a commitment made five years ago but need to be open to the Lord each moment of our lives. I open myself up to the Holy Spirit each day and try to surrender myself to God: in other words, I'm saying to Jesus, "I want to include you in every bit of my existence today."

'It's so important to take practical steps in dealing with any weak area of our lives. I do try to make a conscious decision to bring areas of weakness and failure before Jesus and ask for His help. I recently read a verse from Hosea which initially *made no sense to me: "Ephraim mixes with the nations; Ephraim is a flat cake not turned over" (Hosea 7:8). Reading the notes I was using I began to understand the meaning. A flat cake that isn't turned over only gets cooked on one side. I want to be a person that is exposed to the fire of God on every possible side. I have a passion for IGNITE and my biggest passion is to have Jesus as Lord of my life.*

❗ IGNITE DECLARATION ❗

I commit to: Include Jesus in my moral life, my thoughts, words, actions and relationships.

🔥 FIRESTARTERS 🔥

- If you are in a situation, reading a magazine, watching TV or a video, on the Internet, or in a conversation, and you begin to realise that it's going to affect your thinking, then ask for God's strength to get out straight away.
- Ask Jesus to be at the centre of any new relationships you start. No exclusions.
- When you get money, whether it's weekly or monthly, decide in advance how you are going to use a portion of it for God's kingdom.
- In your daily prayer time, offer to Jesus your talents, your abilities and your future.

4

the best man

I've been privileged to be best man at two different weddings, and it's quite a responsibility. Being the best man at the wedding of my sister Amanda to my best friend Gary was an opportunity to tell all my favourite embarrassing stories about both of them. I remember, too, being the best man at the wedding of our close friends Robert and Janice. All the men were dressed in long coats with tails, a fact I forgot when visiting the toilet just before my speech. Consequently, I sat down on the loo, got the tails of my coat soaking and had to deliver the speech with water dripping down my legs!

The really important thing about being the best man is that you have a close relationship with the groom. I'm sad because I haven't seen for years the friend who was my best man; I still miss his friendship. The bond with the best man is like no other: I can remember my friend Robert, on the night before his wedding, previewing for me his special honeymoon pyjamas and then deciding, with some prompting from me, that perhaps they were a little too tight! What else are friends for? You share stuff with your best man that you wouldn't share with anyone else. It's that type of honour, of intimacy and trust that should mark our relationship with Jesus.

I'm constantly amazed by how much ignorance there is about Jesus. While leading school missions with Big Ideas I come across scores of young people in R.E. lessons who have no real clue about Jesus' life and mission. Sadly, I sometimes come across young people like this in church youth groups too. Gary and I always remember an occasion when we were spending the summer holidays touring from youth camp to youth camp with an evangelistic programme. We included in it a quiz about Jesus which featured the question: 'According to John's Gospel, what were the last three words of Jesus on the cross?' The answer was 'It is finished' but at one camp a young guy stuck his hand up to answer and confidently said, 'I'll be back'! He'd got a bit confused between Jesus and Arnie Schwarzenegger. Of course, The sentiment was the right one, even though the answer was wrong.

Not that I'm saying it's enough to know *about* Jesus instead of actually *knowing* Him. There is no substitute for a personal, daily relationship with Jesus, but how can we develop that intimacy and how can we get closer to Him? We should be people who are constantly moving closer to Jesus and becoming more like Him. If you decide to line up your life to that of Jesus, then you'll find your thinking, your attitudes, your character and actions will begin to match His also. When you hang out with someone all the time you take on their outlook and their characteristics.

Here are three key factors. Once again, each of them really deserves a book but we'll be just covering the tip of the iceberg. Go deeper for yourself. It's time to stop trying to do things *for* God but instead to invest in a relationship *with* God. When God sees that you are serious about this, through being rooted in Scripture and having an intimacy in prayer, then your openness to be guided by the Holy Spirit will increase.

1. Grow closer to Jesus by reading the Bible

One of the phrases Jesus uses most frequently is 'I tell you the truth', and the absolute certainty we have when reading Scripture is that it is truth from God. It's not just about being a biblical scholar, because knowing the book isn't enough – you need to know the author of the book: 'All Scripture is God-breathed and is useful for teaching, rebuking, correcting and training in righteousness' (2 Timothy 3:16). The Bible is the only book in history whose author is present every time it is read! When you read your Bible get ready!

Get ready to hear the truth

Use the Bible as your benchmark for friendship with Jesus and allow it to speak truth into your life. This means taking time to understand what you are reading. There are plenty of good Bible reading schemes and books around. It doesn't matter too much when and how you read the Bible, as long as you do it regularly and with an open heart. If you don't open the Bible willing to hear, then it's a waste of time. If your relationship with Jesus is really going to be intimate, you'll want to read Scripture every day.

Get ready to believe the truth

One of my failings with reading the Bible is that sometimes I do it so quickly and without full concentration that I don't allow quality time for reflection. It's vital to take time to meditate on what you have read and let it sink deep into your mind and soul. This helps so much with 'the renewing of our mind' which we were talking about in the last chapter. Some folk like to establish a regular time and place to read so that they do so expecting to meet with God.

Do not let this Book of the Law depart from your mouth; meditate on it day and night, so that you may be careful to do everything written in it. Then you will be prosperous and successful. (Joshua 1:8)

Get ready to practise the truth

Here's the real challenge! It's not enough to read and believe. If you really want to grow closer to Jesus then your life must be based on the teaching of the Bible and on the example of the life of Jesus you see described in the Bible.

> Do not merely listen to the word, and so deceive yourselves. Do what it says. Anyone who listens to the word but does not do what it says is like a man who looks at his face in a mirror and, after looking at himself, goes away and immediately forgets what he looks like. But the man who looks intently into the perfect law that gives freedom, and continues to do this, not forgetting what he has heard, but doing it – he will be blessed in what he does. (James 1:22–25)

Imagine looking at yourself in a mirror and then immediately forgetting what you look like! In other words, don't let the truth of the Bible go in one ear and out of the other. You have to live out what you hear.

✉ **FROM THE WEB** ✉

'My friend and I started to pray for all our friends in the lunch hour once a week. We've been doing it for two weeks and two people have become Christians already.'

2. Grow closer to Jesus by praying

The great American evangelist, Billy Graham, was once asked by a journalist if he could prove that Jesus was alive. Graham said, 'I know He is alive because I talked to Him this morning.' That is the reality of prayer, a daily opportunity to have a real relationship and conversation with God. You'll have seen the TV adverts for a brand of mobile phone featuring various celebrities describing whom they would most like to have a one-to-one conversation with. Prayer is your incredible gateway into a one-to-one with Jesus.

Most people have prayed at one time or another in their life, perhaps in times of deep distress or incredible joy, even if they didn't really know who they were praying to or if their prayers were going to be heard. I was watching a documentary recently about the British armed forces in the Gulf War. A sergeant was being interviewed and he said that in wartime the chaplain went from being a marginal figure to one of central importance. In the words of the sergeant, most soldiers didn't bother with 'devil dodging' in peacetime, but once at war almost all of them attended services and prayed.

'Jesus' plan for prayer was that it wasn't just for the extreme instances in life but for every part of life. He made it possible for us to converse with God in a real and personal way. Picture the times when you meet your closest friend. The conversation can go on for hours: some of it important, some of it sharing your heartfelt feelings and concerns, some of it fun, some of it seemingly trivial to anyone else who might be listening, some of it meaningless to anyone else but the two of you.

One of the key lessons that Jesus taught about prayer was that it didn't have to be a performance using long, impressive-sounding words or hollow clichés; it just had to be honest and sincere. You have to be yourself when you pray – you don't need big words or a big church. In fact, a great starting point for prayer is somewhere really still and quiet. On holiday in Italy, my wife and I came across a series of meditations around the walls of a church on an island in the middle of a lake. The first sign simply said; 'Silence is meeting with the Master.'

To help His disciples Jesus gave them what has been called the Lord's Prayer. It could just as easily be called the Disciple's Prayer. Why don't you make it your prayer and use it as the basis to ignite your prayer life? Find it in Matthew 6:5–15.

What can we learn from the Lord's Prayer?

God is the centre of your prayer, not you

Jesus starts this prayer by focusing on God and praising the name of His heavenly Father. There are so many aspects of God that deserve your praise and honour, and when you have learnt to move the focus away from yourself and onto God you have learnt an important spiritual lesson for prayer and worship.

God's will is the aim, not your own way

If there was ever someone who might have been justified in following his own instinct, it would have been Jesus. Yet here He demonstrates that God's will is paramount. Just before He is arrested and later crucified Jesus echoes this again, by saying, 'Your will be done.' However enticing it is to use prayer simply to reinforce your own views, if you do so you have missed the point. Prayer is about seeking God's way for your life, not simply telling Him what you want all the time.

God has provided and God will provide

Jesus gives grateful thanks to God for all He has provided and continues by asking God to provide for the future. When you really stop to think about it, the list of items to genuinely thank God for is massive. God cares about your future too, and wants you to explore His will and follow it for the rest of your days. Prayer helps you do that.

God hears prayer and He answers it

Jesus next concentrates on some gigantic issues that cut right to the heart of every person ever born, you included. Everybody needs forgiveness and everyone needs to learn to forgive. Everyone needs guidance and protection. The only person we can completely receive these from is God, and when we ask He hears and He answers. But heed the warning that the heart that is bitter and hard is the heart that God cannot reply to.

God is the first and the last

Jesus finishes the prayer the same way as He starts it – by giving honour and glory to God. When you talk to someone whom you really love and who means everything to you then you'll delight in telling them how great you think they are! Perhaps someone lavishes you with their praise and you know how fantastic that makes you feel. Use your prayers to tell God how absolutely amazing, awesome and mind-blowing He is.

Prayer can help you grow closer to Jesus. Speak to Him every day, make Him your closest and most intimate friend, and listen to what He has to say to you.

✉ **FROM THE WEB** ✉

'I went for the 24/7 prayer. God has really been at work in me coz I don't know what possessed me to say I'd go somewhere on my own and pray for a whole hour. At the time it was a scary prospect – spending so much time with God. But I loved it loads and went again and now I'm praying so much more sincerely. God's love is real to me.'

3. Grow closer to Jesus by the Holy Spirit

Although I'd grown up in church, it wasn't until I went to university that I met Christians who really believed that the Bible was the word of God and who knew an intimacy in prayer. It wasn't until university, too, that I realised I'd grown up worshipping a duo rather than the Trinity. I knew God as Father, Jesus as Lord and Saviour, but I'd never been consciously aware of the Holy Spirit.

Among the Bible study group in my hall of residence I came across people who looked to Scripture for guidance and instruction in life, and who prayed believing God heard and would answer. At one particular meeting, we prayed for an answer to my accommodation problem for the next year. I wanted a place back in halls but there was a waiting list for the one I hoped to be in. The very next day I received a note from the bursar of the hall saying someone had dropped out and I was being offered his room. Coincidence? Well, coincidences like that had never happened to me before.

It was among other Christians that I learnt more and more about the Holy Spirit: Christians who went to different churches than the one I grew up in; Christians who had the power of God present in their daily living. I, on the other hand, believed everything about Christianity, had accepted Jesus and knew I wanted to serve Him, but had a real struggle doing so under my own strength in the tempting world of university life.

In John 13 we see the description of the final days of Jesus' life. Packed into chapter 13 we see Jesus wash his disciples' feet, predict that he is going to be betrayed and also predict that Peter will deny Him. Imagine being a disciple during all this! Your mind would have been in turmoil and you would have been feeling terrible. So in chapter 14 Jesus comforts his disciples with the words: 'Do not let your hearts be troubled. Trust in God; trust also in me' (John 14:1).

He continues by explaining to the disciples that He wouldn't be present in His bodily form for ever but that God the Father would send the Holy Spirit, who would teach and remind people of everything Jesus said: 'And I will ask the Father, and he will give you another Counsellor to be with you for ever – the Spirit of truth' (John 14:16–17).

It's no real surprise to know that the disciples didn't really catch on to what Jesus was talking about. It wasn't to be until the Day of Pentecost in Acts 2 that the followers of Jesus would completely realise that even though Jesus himself had gone to heaven, God would never again leave His people because He would be present in the lives of all believers by the Holy Spirit.

It's through the Holy Spirit that we become Christians in the first place, and it's through the Holy Spirit that we become more like Jesus. When we read the Bible, it is the Holy Spirit that brings it to life and speaks to us through it. When we pray, it is the Holy Spirit who breathes life into our conversation with God. Another sign in the church my wife and I found in Italy simply said, 'Silence is breathing God.' The Greek word *pneuma* and the Hebrew word *ruach* are often translated in Scripture as breath, wind, or Holy Spirit.

The Holy Spirit helps us as we follow Jesus and there is nothing that God can't do in our lives or through us by the power of the Holy Spirit. Another Greek word associated with Spirit is *dunamis* which means power.

There are many learned people who have written great books about the Holy Spirit, but here is a summary for you in four key points:

1. He's a person

Never talk about the Holy Spirit as an 'it' or a 'power'. He is a distinct person. Before the Day of Pentecost, the Spirit of God was *with* the people of God but now He is *in* us. We read earlier that Jesus described the Holy Spirit as the Counsellor: other translations call Him the Friend.

2. He's God

The Holy Spirit is the third person of the Trinity. So he's fully God, and was even present at the creation of the world. So God can live in you and all God's endless potential and power can live in you, too! 'Don't you know that you yourselves are God's temple and that God's Spirit lives in you?' (1 Corinthians 3:16)

3. He's at work today

The Holy Spirit is still at work among Christians and non-Christians alike. He convicts of sin, He prompts us to realise that we are 'horribly distorted and completely unusable' and He gives us the power to change into new creations: 'But when he, the Spirit of truth, comes, he will guide you into all truth' (John 16:13).

The Holy Spirit glorifies Jesus. That's absolutely crucial for you to understand. Whatever denomination or church stream you are a part of, the Holy Spirit should glorify Jesus. If a church or a ministry glorifies itself or a leader, or even the Holy Spirit above Jesus, then you can be sure of one thing – it's not from the Spirit of God. The Holy Spirit glorifies Jesus! He takes from Jesus and gives to you and me, bringing a fresh understanding of spiritual truth from Scripture, helping us with situations we may find ourselves in and developing gifts for us to use serving God. It's the Holy Spirit who brings healing into broken relationships, who acts as our guide when we follow Jesus and who gives us the strength for our journey.

4. He wants to keep on filling you

Whatever your previous experience of the Holy Spirit, and whatever you believe about receiving the Holy Spirit, one thing is certain: He wants to keep filling you with the presence of God every day of your life.

Ephesians 5:18 says: 'Do not get drunk on wine, which leads to debauchery. Instead, be filled with the Spirit.' The phrase in this verse 'be filled with the Spirit' more precisely means 'keep on being filled'. As none of us is perfect, so we are unable to retain the Spirit of God in us in all His fullness. We need to ask constantly for God's Spirit to be present in our lives. Simply put, it's like this – why do we need to keep on being filled? Because we leak! The evangelist J. John often describes how he jumps in the shower first thing in the morning and, as the shower water tumbles down, he asks God to fill him with living water; water that will cleanse, refresh and give new life. Another biblical description of the Spirit is living water. I've adopted that very practical prayer into my life, too. Why don't you do the same?

A life that is filled with power, that defeats the devil, and has good as its priority can be yours. You can know the presence of God by growing closer to Jesus by following the leading of the Holy Spirit.

REAL-LIFE STORY

Laura Picton is 18 and currently on a year-out with Big Ideas before she goes to university.

'Praying has helped me get near to God since I was nine. I got invited to a Daniel prayer group for children and I've been involved ever since. I'm now a leader of a Daniel prayer group

and the oldest person in it. So I've been brought up with prayers that are blunt and honest and simple, and with children who are faithful in prayer and believe it will work.

'There was a time a few years ago when I drifted off in my faith a bit but got back on track thanks to joining a cell group. In fact, I was asked to lead it by the youth leaders at church, and with their support I did lead the cell and enjoyed it. The cell groups were being established after a Big Ideas school mission and up until then the Bible had been a barren land for me, really. I'd seen it as a big, scary book that only a minister could read because it was full of long words for one thing, and ministers always seemed a lot holier than me for another.

'Then I can remember one of the Big Ideas team explain that the Bible was written for me – it was God's letter to me – and I should use it and make it mine. I began to study the Bible at school for A levels and although that meant I got to know John's Gospel and 1 Corinthians very well academically, I used my homework as an excuse not to study the Bible for my own personal growth. I was always too busy, too tired, or had too much homework to read the Bible seriously.

'All that changed a year or so ago when I went on holiday to America with a friend of mine. We did a Bible study together every day and it rocked! The very next week I was away with Big Ideas on a summer team and I had plenty of time each day to get into my Bible. God taught me so much in those three short weeks. I try always to use some Bible reading notes now because this helps me read all the Bible and not just the bits I know. I'd never read the book of Micah, for instance, until I started using the notes someone recently gave me. By the time you read this I'll be well into the IGNITE 'Bible Bits to Ignite your Life' daily readings.

'I aim to read the Bible every day and just love the way God speaks to me through the Psalms in particular. I'm thankful, too, that I have really studied John's Gospel in depth, because I feel like I've really met Jesus closely through it – even if it felt like homework for most of the time!

'I have a number of memories of the Holy Spirit clearly speaking to me through prayer. In fact, one time I had been in bed very ill for two weeks with glandular fever and some important school exams were coming up. All of a sudden one morning I felt fine and got straight up – I later found out my church had been praying for me that same morning!

'Another time in a prayer meeting I had a vision of two loaves, two fishes and some homeless people. A lady in the meeting had the same vision, and to cut a long story short we arranged a Christmas dinner for 150 homeless people in Cardiff as a result of that vision. It was Christmas of 1998 and we approached Harry Ramsden's fish and chip shop in Cardiff Bay. I was a bit afraid because they were a Jewish firm, but the vision from Jesus was so clear. Not only did Harry Ramsden's provide the venue and all the food, but Cardiff Buses provided all the transport to and from Harry Ramsden's for all the homeless.

'I really believe stuff like that happens when you get close to

Jesus. I know that the Holy Spirit is nudging me when I get a gut feeling and know it's Him. More often than not I'll get confirmation in prayer, or from a verse in the Bible, or from another Christian. It's such an amazing feeling when I know that it isn't just my imagination but that Jesus has really spoken to me! A friend of mine recently got his girlfriend pregnant and pretty soon almost everyone deserted him, but as I read the Bible and prayed about him I got a real sense from the Holy Spirit that I should remain his friend and offer him support – I knew that's what Jesus would do.

'I guess everyone has their own style of praying and mine is just talking to Jesus as to my closest friend – because He is! I'm always telling Jesus that He is lush and that he rocks my world! People often come up to me after a prayer meeting and talk about the way I chat with Jesus. I was walking past a church recently and saw that old sign which says, 'Seven days without prayer makes one weak'. I know it's really cheesy but it is so true.

'I was spending one summer working in a shop in Cardiff, and in the first week or so I'm ashamed to say I was so busy and tired again that I left Jesus out of things for a while. Of course, I ended up in a bad way until I went round to a friend's house to pray, read the Bible and sing worship songs. That soon sorted me out!

'Here's my final advice for any young people struggling with some of this stuff. Prayer definitely works – I've just spent two years praying for my friend Katie and seen her come to faith. You can have a real friendship with Jesus as you talk to

*Him. It doesn't matter how you pray, it's the fact that you DO
pray that is important. Remember, too, that the Bible was
written for you, to help you, and that it isn't a big, mysterious
book just for old men. Get a good, recent translation of the
Bible: my favourites are the* Youth Bible *and* The Message.
*When you pray and read the Bible regularly then the Holy
Spirit will begin to rock your world, too!'*

! IGNITE DECLARATION !

I commit to: **G**row closer to Jesus through studying the
Bible, praying and allowing the Holy Spirit to lead me
each day.

🔥 FIRESTARTERS 🔥

- Start the day in the shower (with Living Water)!
- Find a regular place to deepen your relationship
  with Jesus.
- Spend quality time with Him.
- Open the Bible with an expectant heart.
- Remember that silence is meeting with God.
- Remember that silence is breathing in God.
- Make some noise too! Speak out loud to God and
  tell Him how great He is. Use your favourite
  worship CDs to help you focus on Him.

5

you're in the big one!

When I moved down to Cardiff from Surrey, the first thing I did was find a church to join. The second thing I did was find a cricket club to play for. And so for the last 14 years I have played for Lisvane C.C. For the first few years of my membership, the life and soul of the club was its secretary, a legendary man called Bill Ricketts. Whenever I was selected to play for the team, Bill would ring me with the words, 'You're in the Big One!' Whoever we were playing, whatever council-owned pitch we might be playing on, even if our opponents were a scratch team of Bill's mates and we had to bring our own tea, the game was still 'the Big One'. I must admit to enjoying Bill's calls immensely and I allowed myself a moment of pride once I'd heard I was 'in the Big One', even knowing the likelihood was that the game couldn't really be described as 'big' in any shape or form!

I am more and more convinced that one of the main areas we shall be called to account for is our attitude towards other Christians in this world we live in. You and I are 'in the Big One' – the worldwide church – and we should be proud to be part of it, with an urgency to discover who else is part of it too. We shall talk about the local church in more detail in the next chapter, but now we are going to concentrate on developing and maintaining relationships with other Christians.

The apostle Paul challenges us to travel our journey in good relationship with others: 'May the God who gives endurance and encouragement give you a spirit of unity among yourselves as you follow Christ Jesus' (Romans 15:5).

In other words, he's saying, 'You lot should get on with each other as well as Jesus gets on with you all!' Jesus Himself puts it even more strongly. When He prays just before His arrest, He says this:

'My prayer is not for them alone. I pray also for those who will believe in me through their message, that all of them may be one, Father, just as you are in me and I am in you . . . May they be brought to complete unity to let the world know that you sent me and have loved them even as you have loved me.' (John 17:20–23)

So Jesus wants the unity and intimacy that He shares with God the Father to be duplicated by Christians in relationship to one another; for us to be of one heart and of one mind. What practical challenges lay before us, then, to accomplish what Paul and Jesus so passionately desire for all believers?

1. The church is in my town or city

In the New Testament, churches are almost always referred to as the group of believers in a particular city, such as Corinth, Ephesus, Rome and Philippi. Even when Paul writes to a group of churches, such as in Galatia, he writes one letter to them all. With our modern-day denominations and streams of church we have forgotten the city-wide emphasis of the early church. God is interested in towns and cities. Just as Jesus looked over Jerusalem and wept, I believe he looks over the towns and cities that you and I live in and experiences similar emotions.

Sadly, for too long Christians have looked over towns and cities and been more concerned about competing with other churches and allowing a suspicion, jealousy and separation to breed. That must break God's heart, and one of the exciting factors about the launch of IGNITE in Cardiff and the surrounding area is that young people are beginning to break down barriers between churches and build up relationships that cross traditional boundaries of theology and denomination.

When Big Ideas launched IGNITE in the summer of 2000, we invited church leaders from across the city to join us in the Cardiff Bay visitors' centre. During the evening together, we gathered round a board map of the city and prayed for the city, its leadership, young people and our churches. We asked Jesus to have mercy on Cardiff. Over 70 leaders from 30 different churches were present. One friend of mine, actually on the board of trustees for Big Ideas, confided that he hadn't seen one of the other leaders there since they were in a youth group together 30 years ago. They had ended up at different churches, and it wasn't that they'd fallen out, just that they hadn't really mixed since their teenage years!

Five days after that launch for leaders, over 100 young people gathered on the top of Garth Mountain, just outside of Cardiff, and while the rain pelted down we again prayed for Cardiff. We weren't due to launch IGNITE officially for young people for three months, but we all prayed that 'the new IGNITE thing' would really be used by God to impact Cardiff and the surrounding area. By Christmas 2000, just three months after the IGNITE initiative was launched, we had over 500 young people signed up to the declaration and they represented nearly 80 churches! Suddenly, the beginnings of city-wide trust and relationship, in the early stages with church leaders, were being overtaken by an emerging generation.

You will do well if you remember this: your local church is where your most important relationships, after God and family, should be. It's there that you will find the accountability and authenticity that you will need to grow as a follower of Jesus. The next chapter will take you deeper into the local church.

✉ **FROM THE WEB** ✉

'I've just returned from an absolutely fantastic weekend away, in which God has moved in amazing and powerful ways. It was incredible to meet up with other "on fire" Christians. One thing God spoke to me about was that we need to get out of our comfort zone and get dangerous. We need to get out there where the hungry and lost are, where the hungry and thirsty for Jesus are. We need to be guilty of being on fire and setting others on fire. COME ON let's be arsonists and set these people on fire. U WITH ME?'

---

2. The church is in my country

I've recently turned 40 and my brother-in-law Gary mentioned that he thought I'd escaped a mid-life crisis until he borrowed my car. There he found a selection of freshly recorded cassette tapes of all my favourite Christian bands from the 1980s! I'd decided eventually to transfer some of my old vinyl albums to tape, and Gary had taken that as a sign of me wanting to live in the past. I prefer to look at it as a tribute to the influence bands and artists, such as After the Fire, Bryn Haworth, 100% Proof and Steve Taylor, had on me. (I know you have never heard of these dinosaurs!) More important, perhaps, was the influence that the places where I heard these bands had on me.

Every summer without fail, in my older teens and twenties, I would squeeze a load of people into my car and head to the Greenbelt Christian arts festival. If you wanted to see bands, that was the place – there was no Soul Survivor or anything else like it in those days. I often saw these bands and other Christian performers at university too, and began to travel to other one-off events and concerts. Without actually realising it I was tapping into the wider UK church and beginning to hear leaders and speakers of influence. At these gatherings I met Christians my own age from all over the UK.

Today, there are many opportunities to go to Bible weeks, festivals or Christian holidays and have your perspective on the church raised. Perhaps you do that regularly and enjoy the friendship of people from different parts of the country and from different churches. I'm not suggesting you develop an event mentality, where you lurch from the emotional high of one event into the depression of being back at home and then off to the next event and the next emotional high. You can't live a life just on the mountain top experiences. I would say, though, that regional and national events, especially geared to young people, will encourage you, challenge you and allow you to meet up with God's church in this country!

In the book of Revelation we read that one day in heaven people from *every nation* will be standing before the throne worshipping. That includes the nation we live in, so God has a plan for it and He wants you to be part of that plan. Being privileged to travel around the UK with Big Ideas, I am able to meet up with folk from all over, and I feel encouraged, excited and challenged when friends tell me what God is getting up to in their town and in their church.

3. The church is in my world

If the world were a village of 1,000 people then 329 of them would be Christians! We live in what many people call the global village, and with the wonders of modern transport and communication we are able to enjoy relationships with Christians around the world like never before in history. When ordinary Christians become brave enough to step out of their own comfort zone and start getting involved in the body of Christ overseas then God blesses that: 'The LORD had said to Abram, "Leave your country, your people and your father's household and go to the land I will show you. I will make you into a great nation and I will bless you"' (Genesis 12:1–2).

I've been greatly blessed by God when I've travelled overseas and worked with Christians and churches in different countries. (In fact, I'm writing this chapter sitting in the home of Russ and Lara, who are youth pastors in Fort Wayne, Indiana, USA.) What has left a lasting impression on me has been the faith and commitment of the Christians that I have met. Over a period of about ten years, I have been the manager of Christians in Sport cricket tours to places like South Africa, Zimbabwe and India. Organised by Andrew Wingfield Digby from Christians in Sport, these tours have had the aims of supporting evangelistic sports ministry, working with local churches, and fundraising for worthwhile projects, all in the framework of playing good quality cricket.

Staying in a hotel in Hyderabad, India, on one such trip I was asked to speak at a church on the other side of the city. The pastor of the church was also the doorman at our hotel, and he agreed to collect me at 9.00 a.m. on the Sunday morning. Only when I met him at 9.00 a.m. did I realise two things: first, he always worked all night through on a Saturday, so he hadn't had any sleep, and second, our journey was to be on his moped! It was a regular Sunday journey for him, as he always led the morning service despite no sleep, and we arrived safely at his church, which was, in fact, a large tarpaulin stretched between four wooden poles in the back garden of a lady's house. There were 40 or 50 people sheltered from the sun to hear me speak. After the pastor dropped me back at the hotel, he went back to the church until his evening shift was due to start again. He made no great show of his dedication: it was the norm for him.

On another occasion in Harare, Zimbabwe, I had arranged to meet a young youth worker from The Boys' Brigade in Zimbabwe in his office on a Monday morning. I took along with me some of our cricket team, professional players from the UK, as we were planning to raise some money to help with providing a well for the water supply at a campsite run by The Boys' Brigade. We arrived at the office about 10.30 a.m. and met the young man. He had been organising a leadership training course that weekend in the countryside outside Harare. The venue had been over 40 kilometres away. The course finished too late for him to catch a bus back into the city and unfortunately the vehicle provided by his employers, a moped again, had a punctured tyre – and there was no money available to mend it. Rather than stay overnight, he decided to walk back to the city so that he would not miss our visit. He arrived home from his walk at 5.00 a.m. and went into his office at 7.30 a.m., just in case we arrived early. His story, again told with no hint of pride, was a humbling experience for those of us listening. At the time, I did a similar job to him in the UK, and was provided with a company car with a servicing agreement and a credit card for my travel expenses.

Recently, I travelled into Scandinavia with singer-songwriter Eli, and our experiences there confirmed to me the truth of this chapter. For a start, there we were, an American born in Los Angeles and living in Nashville (Eli) and a British guy born near London and living in Cardiff (me), ministering together in Norway, Sweden and Denmark. We were constantly grateful to God for the opportunity He had given us, and we were consistently blessed by the other Christians that we met on our whirlwind six-day trip.

For a start, I was collected at Oslo airport by a young Norwegian called Johann. His parents were Koreans and had been living in Norway for many years. His father was a pastor and was so respected that he was the first contact for many Koreans coming into Norway. Johann had recently been studying in the UK and was now back, working with a Teen Challenge project in Oslo until he started university. On the way to our first venue we also collected a girl called Jemma. She also worked with Teen Challenge and was from the Philippines.

She had originally been to Norway on a mission trip and had come back long-term to work with drug addicts, prostitutes and homeless people, on the streets of Oslo. Her enthusiasm for ministry and love for Jesus overwhelmed me. When I said to her that it was a tragedy that in every city in the world you could find homeless people, drug addicts and prostitutes, she simply said that in every city you would find Christians standing alongside them, sharing God's love. What a great outlook!

Then I met another Teen Challenge leader, who told me of the growing ministry to teenagers that was being launched from Norway into Russia and the Baltic states. In Sweden I spent time talking and praying with a young South African called Chris, who also stayed on in Norway after an initial mission trip. He had brought his youth group over to the Swedish Christian festival that Eli was playing at. Chris was planning to produce a youth friendly version of the Bible in Norwegian. I was humbled as we prayed together and for each other.

When we arrived in Denmark, Eli and I spent a few hours with a man called Alan. Every now and then I believe God gives us a special connection with someone else in the body of Christ. Alan was a lecturer to worship leaders at the college we were visiting. He also ran a worship record label and was soon to go back into a massive church in Copenhagen as a worship pastor himself. Alan, Eli and I soon realised that God had given us the same heart for young people, discipleship, worship and contemporary Christian music. Just meeting Alan sent me back to my hotel room thrilled.

Then, next day at the concert, Eli introduced me to

four friends of his from previous trips to Denmark. These guys had set up a demonstration against a Christian festival Eli had played at a few years before. They had played their thrash metal CDs as loud as they could nearby and regularly dropped their trousers to any Christians who passed them. Eli had dared to go over to them and, rather than complain, simply began to talk to them. To cut a long story short, the next time Eli played at that festival, those four guys were in attendance – not demonstrating against it! When I met them, they were so thrilled at meeting up with Eli again and came into his concert. Those guys aren't Christians yet, but their lives are already changing and they are comfortable in a Christian environment that a few years before they would have been deriding and belittling.

I've tried to keep in contact with Christians I have met overseas, and with friends who are serving God in different parts of the world; I enjoy receiving their prayer letters. Following the prompting of the Holy Spirit, I have also committed to financially support overseas mission work.

Similarly, I have seen great blessing when hosting Christians from overseas. My wife and I have just had a young married couple (Russ and Lara) from America staying with us for two weeks, and it was a joy to get to know them, to pray together and to dream dreams for the future together. During the Rugby World Cup in Cardiff in November 1999, Big Ideas co-ordinated a visit by a group of South African rugby coaches from SCAS (Sports for Christ Action South Africa). They were led by Frans Cronje (you may recognise the surname – his brother Hansie was the South African cricket captain), and they worked with churches, schools and rugby clubs for a three-week period during the World Cup.

So successful was the trip, and such an impact did they make everywhere they went, that we are in the process of arranging their third trip in three years back to South Wales. Frans Cronje became a close friend and was a special help to our cricket tour to South Africa early in 2000. For me, it was a thrill to share gospel ministry with Frans on both sides of the world – in his city and in mine.

Hopefully, you will already have your own stories of friendships with Christians from around the world. If you haven't, then how about praying that God will begin to develop these relationships as you serve Him? When you meet Christians from a different place than you come from, there can only be one result: God stirs a passion and a fire in your heart. Wherever we are in the world, when we risk building relationships then God blesses them.

REAL-LIFE STORY

Pete Joyce is 19 at the time of writing and currently completing 18 months working with Big Ideas.

'When I was little I went to Sunday school, but I stopped when I was about eleven. I got on with regular school life, but generally things didn't go too well: my exam results were bad, I was insecure, and became increasingly worried about the future. I left school with poor qualifications and not many friends.

'Then one of the few friends I did have invited me to a café evening that Big Ideas were running. There was live music, good coffee and an opportunity to meet new people. The café ran for ten weeks and I went along each week, but whenever a speaker got up I used to sneak off down to the chip shop. One week, Nigel spotted me and before I could go out he suggested I sit down and listen. So I sat down among a small group of teenagers and listened to their discussions about being a Christian. In fact, I met up with them in a cell group for months afterwards, too. I'd found people who accepted me; I had a sense of belonging and I was part of a community. It wasn't long before I became a Christian, found a local church and got baptised.

'Three years on I have lots of friends – Christian friends from churches all over Cardiff. It's really exciting. Now the list of numbers in my mobile phone is so full I have a real dilemma about who to delete to put a new name in! It's an absolute nightmare! Seriously though, it's encouraging to have mates from all over the place. I have some very close friends who I'm accountable to, who build me up in my Christian walk as I share my life with them. Everybody knows me for my catch-phrase, "You beauty"!

'I love the opportunity to be part of IGNITE events now because I want to see young people experience the same sense of belonging to Jesus, of community together, that I experience. I guess that's why I give some of my time to work on the St Mellons estate in Cardiff, too. It's not really my ideal venue for a great night out – in fact, it's a very tough estate, with many social problems – but my friends and I support a local church project there because we want to see teenagers on that estate reached with the good news of Jesus, and we want to serve God. Our dance nights give teenagers a chance to enjoy themselves in a safe environment and be shown genuine care and love from Christians.

'As well as local stuff, I love going to national stuff too. Every time I go to Soul Survivor, for instance, I feel God light a fire in me. I get spiritually refreshed and excited about my faith all over again. It's the encouragement of being part of thousands of young people from all over the UK who are the same as me. I even bump into people from Cardiff I haven't met before – nightmare! Where do I put them in my mobile phone?

'I really believe the time I have spent working with Big Ideas is where God has wanted me to be. Part of my experience has involved travelling with our school mission team to places such as Milton Keynes, Weymouth, Bournemouth and Kingham Hill in Oxfordshire. I must admit that it has been a bit scary going off to a place I've never been before, to work in a school for a week and to stay with people I haven't met before. Yet God is in control, and I arrive back in Cardiff each time having gained new friends and more opportunities to serve God.

'Another aspect of my time with Big Ideas has been to look after overseas visitors when they come to Cardiff to minister alongside us. Over the last year or so, my understanding of the worldwide church has been increased since I've met Christian young people from other countries. I still have vivid memories of spending time with a group of South Africans who came over to coach rugby and share their faith, and of meeting up with one American band in particular. I was able to show them the sights a bit as we talked about our life as Christians.

'The highlight of my time with Big Ideas has to be the first IGNITE overseas mission trip to Amsterdam. At Easter 2001, a team of eight of us spent ten days in Amsterdam working with a local church there. Our aim was to develop relationships with children and young people on the streets and bring them into the environment of the church.

'I was really nervous before we went; in fact, I was petrified, but God was faithful and we had an amazing time. God was at work in the lives of many young people we met, and in our lives too. It was so cool to meet Christian leaders in Holland and to work with them and learn from them. I will always remember how they served God in their culture powerfully and effectively, and felt privileged to help them.

'I suppose that the church I am part of in Cardiff is a fair reflection of what I'm trying to say. City Temple is a church which has people attending from all over Cardiff, and also students and families from all over the world. The church is *really building me up and giving me further opportunities to serve the kingdom, not least because of the sheer variety of people there.'*

IGNITE DECLARATION

I commit to: **N**etwork with other Christians in my city, my country and throughout the world.

FIRESTARTERS

City

● Get involved in a local church.

● Seek out good Christian friends.

● Support the Christian Union at your school or college.

● Don't criticise churches or church members – yours or anyone else's.

Country

● Go to large-scale events and take your youth group with you.

● Seek out Christian friends from around the UK.

● Take your experiences back to your local church (but do it gently!).

World

● Go on an overseas mission trip.

- Support financially an overseas project.
- Host a team of Christians from overseas.
- Develop an exchange partnership with Christians from another country.
- Seek out Christian friends from around the world.

6

perfect attendance?

What kept me going to church when I was young was the fact that I was involved in The Boys' Brigade. The object of the organisation was the advancement of Christ's kingdom, but I must admit that what attracted me to start with was the football team, the marching band and the summer camp. You couldn't play football for the team if you didn't go to church the previous week!

If you never missed a Friday night meeting or Bible class on a Sunday for a whole year you got a Perfect Attendance award. When I was about 14, I got one! I wouldn't say my attendance at church has been perfect since then, or that the four churches I've been a member of since were perfect, but I'm completely committed to the life of the local church. Being part of a church brings joys and frustrations, but there is no alternative! Paul reminds us of our membership and responsibility: 'Now you are the body of Christ, and each one of you is a part of it' (1 Corinthians 12:27).

Our first responsibility to the church must be locally, where we commit to meet regularly and share life with other believers. Whatever our thoughts about church tradition or denomination, we must have that local relationship with the body of Christ. Nowhere in the Bible does it talk about 'church' meaning a place or a building, but instead it talks about a group or body of people – believers in Jesus Christ – who are called together by God.

When I was in South Africa with Christians in Sport, four of us visited Robben Island off Cape Town, where Nelson Mandela had been held captive for so many years. Among our group was Devon Malcolm, the England cricketer, who had met Mandela on a number of occasions and who was something of a legend in South Africa after his exploits on the field against the South Africans for England, and because he was black himself.

It was an emotional time for Devon to see Mandela's cell and the courtyard where he exercised, but the most poignant part of our tour of the island was when we were taken into a limestone quarry. Our guide pointed to a cave at one end of the quarry and said that it was meant just to be a place for the prisoners to use as a toilet. However, in the winter they gathered in there to keep warm; in the summer they gathered there to shelter from the sun, and the guide said that the cave became whatever those prisoners wanted it to be – schoolhouse, community centre, government building. In fact, most of Nelson Mandela's first government frequented that cave.

You see, it didn't matter to them that the cave was supposed to be just a toilet – the building itself wasn't important, but what was important was the vision and the attitude of the people who met there. Sitting on our guided tour bus and allowing the guides words to sink in, I realised that this was a fantastic model of what church should be: not constrained by buildings but based on the common journey and relationships of those who are part of it. It always seems strange to me that, although we know church should be about people and not buildings, we so often act as if the opposite were true!

Some years ago, my wife Gill and I were fortunate to receive two free flights to America, courtesy of buying an electrical appliance from a well-known retailer. We had never been to America before and chose to go to New York. When we were there, as well as doing all the tourist stuff, we visited some churches. The gospel choir in the church in Harlem had to be seen and heard to be believed, but what really struck us was the contrast between two other churches we went to. The first was the cathedral church of St John the Divine, an Episcopalian church in Amsterdam Avenue, which is at the top of Central Park, near to Harlem. It is home to various civic ceremonies and houses a vast array of priceless tapestries and artefacts from the Vatican.

The building was built in 1892 but it is still not finished – cynics say that is because unfinished buildings don't pay city tax. To leave the church on a weekday tour you have to go through its gift shop, and on the way out you pass homeless people begging for a few cents. We felt distinctly uneasy about the opulence and luxury of the church inside and the presence of poverty-stricken folk on its doorstep.

Then we visited Times Square church, the home of David Wilkerson of *The Cross and the Switchblade* and Nicky Cruz fame. This church was in an old Broadway theatre, had a team of smartly blazered ushers and an incredible band of musicians on the stage. Yet the lasting impression was from the people sitting near to us. In our row we discovered policemen and doctors worshipping alongside ex-drug addicts and prostitutes. We found out the service was being simultaneously translated into four different languages so that the Hispanics, Chinese, Italians and others around us could hear the sermon in their native language. Every night of the week the church had a bus patrolling the streets of New York, offering medication, food and hope to addicts and homeless people, and also ran discipleship groups in a variety of languages. For the rest of our time in New York, we wondered what God felt about those two different churches, and which one came closest to matching the biblical model of church.

Simply speaking, the church is all about people and following Jesus and being committed to share that journey with each other. You will never grow as a Christian in isolation. Hopping from church to church with no real depth of relationship is of little help either. Some of you reading this might already be disillusioned with church and you might have decided to opt out of church altogether. Others of you might be struggling to find a newer and more relevant model of church for your generation. Whatever your relationship to church at the moment, be certain of this: to represent Jesus effectively on this earth you have to be a part of the group of His followers called 'church'. By looking at the Bible you can discover the reasons why you need to be involved in the church.

The church is a body

There is a place for everyone in the church, and everybody has a part to play. It is the body of Christ on earth and has the challenge of carrying His work on. Some people think that being one body means that we all have to be the same, but that is not true at all:

Just as each of us has one body with many members, and
these members do not all have the same function, so in
Christ we who are many form one body, and each member
belongs to all the others. (Romans 12:4–5)

I sometimes imagine what part of the body I should be
– perhaps the little toe, or the belly button, or an ear
lobe, or even an appendix! You get the idea – without
every little bit, the body isn't a complete body. You
know that every bit of your body is vitally important to
you. There might be some bits you'd like to improve,
but you wouldn't want to be without them.

We don't have to be the same as every other part in
the body, but we do have a responsibility to the other
parts of the body. If you choose to opt out of church
you are in effect saying, 'I don't want to be a part of the
body of Christ on earth.' Body life comes through Jesus
and nothing else. All the meetings, programmes,
buildings and plans of the church mean nothing unless
the Holy Spirit moves through them. If you go it alone,
either as churches without Jesus being the centre, or as
individual people trying to live as Christians without
others, then you will fail: 'I am the vine; you are the
branches. If a man remains in me and I in him, he will
bear much fruit; apart from me you can do nothing'
(John 15:5).

So if you try to remain on fire for God separately from
church, first you will miss out on real body life, and

second, the church will miss out on the unique contribution only you can make to the body!

The church is an army

There is no doubt that you have been called to take your place in the battle against injustice and inequality, to wage war against sin and the powers of darkness: 'Endure hardship with us like a good soldier of Christ Jesus' (2 Timothy 2:3).

In other words, in one way or another we have to be front-line troops, and the best way to be a soldier is to fight alongside other people. There is one famous story of a Japanese soldier who remained in isolation in the jungle years after the Second World War ended. No one told him it had finished, so he carried on thinking he was at war and was eventually found 30 or so years later, a confused, bedraggled madman. Imagine how soul-destroying it must have been for him, believing he was at war but being totally alone. You are not alone in your fight and God has never asked you to be alone in your fight: the Holy Spirit lives in you and God has put other Christians in the front line with you.

The church is pioneering

You can be part of God's plan to bring change into a world that is hurting and aimless without Jesus.

> These twelve Jesus sent out with the following instructions: 'Do not go among the Gentiles or enter any town of the Samaritans. Go rather to the lost sheep of Israel. As you go, preach this message: "The kingdom of heaven is near." Heal the sick, raise the dead, cleanse those who have leprosy, drive out demons. Freely you have received, freely give.' (Matthew 10:5–8)

If you aren't moving forwards, then, by definition, you are moving backwards. In church life there is no such thing as standing still. You aren't called to settle down, to prevent change and to resist anything new: in fact you are called to be exactly the opposite. The church of Jesus today needs people who are pioneers to remain in the body and help move the church in the direction God wants it to travel. You could be one of those pioneers! The church of the future is going to look radically different from the way it does now, and you can be one of the people who will shape the church for years to come. The church needs your commitment, your passion, your vision and your presence.

The church is a family

Meaningful relationships which transcend generation, gender and race should genuinely be found in the church. It is the family of God: 'Yet to all who received him, to those who believed in his name, he gave the right to become children of God' (John 1:12).

Throughout history, many people who feel isolated and unloved in the world have found a real sense of belonging and of family for the first time when they join a church. That is no real surprise, because that's what the church is supposed to be like.

In these days of rapidly shifting patterns of church life, with older denominations struggling and various youth churches emerging alongside newer models of church, what should your criteria be for church life? What should we look for in this family? Here are some suggestions. Remember, we are talking about people and not places.

Are you travelling in the same direction?

The Message translation of the Bible sums this up

superbly in Ephesians 4 by saying: 'You were all called to travel on the same road and in the same direction, so stay together, both outwardly and inwardly.'

There needs to be a sense of unity in church and a shared vision. Being willing to follow God's appointed leaders is vital so that you know you are going in the direction God wants you to. Too many churches waste energy and dishonour God by arguing among themselves as to what their priorities should be. A church that is united behind its leadership, under God, is a powerful church.

Coming back from university to my home church, I made the mistake of thinking I knew everything about church from my new experiences at university. Whether I was right or not, my outspokenness wasn't respectful to the leadership of the church and caused irritation to many and frustration to me. Eventually, I realised the error of my ways and gracefully moved onto another church.

I don't suggest you repeat my mistake. Since then, I've tried to be a part of the vision of each church I've been a member of and support the leadership:

Obey your leaders and submit to their authority. They keep watch over you as men who must give an account. Obey them so that their work will be a joy, not a burden, for that would be of no advantage to you. (Hebrews 13:17)

Try to take on the perspective that when a church leader is speaking to you or asking you to get involved in something, it's Jesus Himself speaking!

Are you travelling together?

Your point of reference for church today is always the early church:

> They devoted themselves to the apostles' teaching and to the fellowship, to the breaking of bread and to prayer. Everyone was filled with awe, and many wonders and miraculous signs were done by the apostles. (Acts 2:42–43)

One step on from unity is community. A real and obvious sense of care and value for each other is vital. You need to belong to your church, not just by signing a piece of paper or receiving a handshake in a service but actually *knowing and feeling* that you belong. In this age, many people want to have a community to belong to even before they are ready to believe everything that the community believes. I knew I belonged to the church, because I was part of the community of young people who played football and went to camp even before I became a Christian. Church should be the place where, above every other place, even your own family, you can truly say, 'I belong.' That's the type of community that will attract others.

Can anyone travel with you?

Alongside unity and community there must be room for diversity. Is there a place for all backgrounds, all nationalities and races, all ages and all experiences? Once again, *The Message* translation sums this up perfectly from Acts 10 in Peter's vision: 'God plays no favorites! It makes no difference who you are or where you're from . . .'

While I understand the need for youth churches and see how they have grown, I have concerns about them. Some church leaders look into the future and predict more and more fragmentation of churches – separate congregations for young people, business people, families, etc. The way the Times Square church catered for all the variety of people in New York has remained with me as an example of how church can be.

One final image from the Bible concerning church is that of the bride of Christ. Jesus is described as the Bridegroom who will one day return to claim His bride: 'I saw the Holy City, the new Jerusalem, coming down out of heaven from God, prepared as a bride beautifully dressed for her husband' (Revelation 21:2). If and when you get married, you will experience the expectancy and anticipation of the wedding day and of finally marrying your beloved. Imagine the anticipation and expectancy of the bride of Christ meeting Jesus. Perhaps your main reason for being committed to the church is that you will be among the people and in the place where Jesus shall expect to find you!

Going to church on a Sunday

Having said all through this chapter that church is about people and not a building, most of you will worship in a church on a Sunday that meets in a building of some description. How you actually approach the act of going to church is crucially important to how you grow closer to Jesus.

Picture the scene in my house on a Sunday morning: I wake up full of good intentions, realise it's Sunday and decide to have a bit of a lie-in before getting up. After showering, I rush downstairs to grab some breakfast and then wait for my wife to finish preparing stuff for the Sunday lunch before we jump in the car with our daughter and head off to church.

If the traffic is OK and we can get a parking space, we arrive in church in time for the welcome at the start of the service; if not, we arrive in the first song. I spend half the service focused on what's happening and half on what I'm up to for the rest of the day. Then, after a quick coffee in the foyer, we dash back home for dinner and then I collapse in front of the TV and read the paper.

OK, I exaggerate! But it is like that sometimes, and for any of you who can associate with that, then let me tell you that if we don't prepare well for church and give it thought afterwards too, then we might as well not bother going. In 2 Chronicles 29 you can find the story of Hezekiah rebuilding the Temple. It had got into a state of disrepair and wasn't being used. Of course, that meant the people weren't worshipping. So Hezekiah rebuilds, reopens and recommissions the Temple of the Lord. This is what Hezekiah says to the people:

> Then Hezekiah said, 'You have now dedicated yourselves to the LORD. Come and bring sacrifices and thank-offerings to the temple of the LORD.' So the assembly brought sacrifices and thank-offerings, and all whose hearts were willing brought burnt offerings. (2 Chronicles 29:31)

You can see that their response centred on having willing hearts. This is the exact attitude for church. I confess that there was a time a few years ago where my own attendance at church had purely become a sense of duty – I was only going because I'd feel guilty if I didn't. Since then I've had to ask God's forgiveness and put my heart attitude to church in order. Your heart must be 'willing' to go to church. You need an air of expectancy before you attend on a Sunday, and a time of reflection after you have been. Church, above everything else, is where you will meet with the people of God, worship God together and hear Him speak into your life. To allow the Holy Spirit to have maximum impact in those areas, you'll need to give church more than an hour or so. Your willing heart should be open to church from the moment you awake on a Sunday until the moment you go to sleep.

REAL-LIFE STORY

Paul Reed is 20 and currently works for Big Ideas on the IGNITE initiative.

'My family are from a church background, and when I was seven we moved house and started going to the church we are members of now. My mum and dad had attended different churches and liked Bethesda Chapel in Dinas Powis, so that's where we are.

'I can remember making a step of faith at the age of nine at a camp, which helped me keep on going to church. By the age of 14 I was listening and learning more, but by the age of 18 I really wanted to leave the church. I just felt that there was nothing for me and that I didn't have a role to play in the church.

'I told my parents and obviously they were very upset, but I kept saying, "I'm going to leave and go to another church." My parents pleaded with me to give the church one more chance and to try getting involved a bit more. The very next Sunday I reluctantly went to church and was asked to think about becoming a youth leader. To this day I'm convinced my

mum and dad hadn't said anything to anyone! I immediately felt God was giving me some guidance and so I agreed to help with the younger teenagers.

'It was the best thing I could have done and now nearly three years on, I really love working with the over twelves. It's so much fun helping them that I willingly give up my time with my own friends to concentrate on these younger people. As well as spending time with them and learning to relate to them, I do see them respond to me when we get down to more serious stuff.

'I now go to church to grow spiritually. I value the service, the youth group, the cell group and the Bible study. I'm determined to learn more from the Bible, to adjust my attitudes in life, and I want to help others to learn too.

'I've got a wide circle of friends from different churches in and around Cardiff, and I'm sometimes tempted to go to their church if it is bigger or seen to be more popular than mine. But I know God has called me to be part of my church.

'In the last year or so, our church has appointed two new elders. There had been a feeling that the elders were untouchable and unapproachable, but I asked if I could meet with them to hear about their vision for the church. They spoke clearly to me about their hopes and dreams for the future. I was really pleased to say to them that I was ready to be a part of their future vision. I had been baptised in 1997 and joined the fellowship soon afterwards, but nevertheless wanted to show personally to the church leadership that I valued them and supported them.

'If I ever move away from Dinas Powis, there are a number of things I would look for in a church. I would want to benefit from good and enthusiastic Bible-based teaching. I would want to see and be a part of a vision to reach out to non-Christians in the local area. And I'd want to experience God in worship that is real and alive.

'As I read the Bible and see the early church in action, I constantly marvel at the togetherness and fellowship of the early church life – the unity of the people across a city-wide area. I'm beginning to see that no church is bigger than the kingdom of God. IGNITE has done so much to help churches across Cardiff and the surrounding area, and to encourage young people to get involved. The church of the twenty-first century has to be contemporary and relevant and must respond to changing culture. IGNITE does just that and encourages churches to do the same.'

❢ IGNITE DECLARATION ❢

I commit to: Involve myself in a local church and respect its leadership.

🔥 FIRESTARTERS 🔥

- Don't just *go* to church, but *commit* to one.
- Get to know members of your church who are a different age than you (invite them to meet the youth group).
- Listen to your church leaders.
- Pray for them.
- Listen to your youth leaders.
- Pray for them.
- Ask yourself this question, 'How can I support my church more effectively?'

7

step up to the microphone

Stepping up

In my front room at home I have a 1950s-style microphone, mounted as a trophy, with an inscription on it. It was given to me by the band Newsboys for speaking each night on their 'Step up to the Microphone' tour at the end of 1998 and into 1999. In 60 cities I stepped up to the microphone to challenge

American teenagers to give up a summer to travel on a mission trip.

Stepping up to the microphone is a good way of looking at the challenge Jesus gives to each of us. Being a Christian means that each of you will definitely be called to 'step up to the microphone' in one way or another. Some of you who read this book will become evangelists, missionaries, pastors, preachers or church leaders. Others of you will be God's spokesmen and women in the world of education, or business or medicine. Some of you will be naturally good public speakers and will relish the call of God on your life to speak – in fact, people will struggle to shut you up! For others of you, the whole concept of being public and outspoken about your faith sends a shiver down your spine.

But here's the deal: all of you have been called to be a witness for Jesus, and he demands from you not just words but a lifestyle too. So we are not going to limit 'stepping up to the microphone' with words only. The challenges of this chapter are how and why we should share our faith not just by what we say but by what we do also: 'But you will receive power when the Holy Spirit comes on you; and you will be my witnesses in Jerusalem, and in all Judea and Samaria, and to the ends of the earth' (Acts 1:8).

It's simple

One of my favourite little stories is about a shy monk. You might well have heard this story before. I first heard it 20 years ago from two different preachers in the same church two weeks running! The shy monk is in a monastery, and the abbot is the head of the monastery. He comes up to the monk and tells him that he will have to speak in the chapel one morning. The shy monk protests, but still finds himself in front of all the other monks one morning. With trembling knees and a beating heart he steps up to the microphone and says to the gathering, 'Do you know what I'm going to say?' All the other monks chorus back, 'No.' 'Nor do I,' says the monk and runs back to his seat. He's really embarrassed but reckons at least he'll never have to speak in chapel again.

He can hardly believe it when a few weeks later he is ordered to speak again, and despite more protest, has to go through with it. Extremely nervous, he steps up to the microphone for a second time and says, 'Do you know what I am going to say?' All the other monks reply together, 'Yes,' so the shy monk says, 'Well, there is no need for me to tell you then,' and runs off, humiliated again, but at least he thinks to himself that he has escaped speaking in chapel for ever.

Imagine his complete surprise and panic when, for a third time, he is ordered to speak in the chapel service.

The abbot has been strangely silent about his first two efforts and is determined for him to speak again. So yet again the shy monk finds himself stepping up to the microphone: 'Do you know what I'm going to say?' he starts once more. Now half the monks reply, 'No' and the other half reply, 'Yes'. 'Right,' says the shy monk, 'those of you who know tell those of you who don't' and then runs off.

To his surprise he is overtaken by the abbot, who says to him, 'What a fantastic message, and so simple: "Those of you who know tell those of you who don't." What a great call to share our faith.'

What witnessing boils down to is that simple message: those of us who know Jesus should share Him with people who don't. We must do that with our words, our actions, our complete lives.

Let love be your energy

For many years I used to think that the most important thing to help us witness was to have a plan or a strategy – both individually and as a church. You know the stuff I'm talking about: a well thought-out testimony and gospel presentation to use, and a plan to reach all the homes in the neighbourhood around the church. Just recently, I've come to the conclusion that at best strategy is only the second most important thing. Reading Luke chapter 15, where we see the stories of the lost coin, the lost sheep, and the lost son, I realised that Jesus is talking about having a consistent and persistent love for the lost.

However many evangelism strategies we have, however many outreach programmes we put into place, however much we talk about personal witnessing, unless we desperately love and compassionately search for people who are spiritually lost then our efforts lack the right motivation. To put it simply: if we want to witness effectively, we have got to love people. God's love for us, and His desire to share that with others, must be at the bottom of all we do. Those of us who know should tell those of us who don't because God's love is so incredible in our lives we would hate for anyone else to miss it; we can't bear to see people around us lose the opportunity to know God's love for themselves!

Of course, it is absolutely useless to talk about love but not demonstrate it in your life. You will probably know that one of the biggest criticisms levelled at us Christians is the word 'hypocrite'. In other words, people aren't prepared to listen to our words if our lives don't match up. The world we live in needs to see you and me living out our faith as much as talking about it. So don't think that stepping up to the microphone is all about words: it's so much more.

I recently heard a great story about Pepsico – the American company that makes Pepsi Cola. They had launched a series of TV adverts promoting a voucher that you got if you bought Pepsi drinks. For every ten vouchers you could send away for a T-shirt; for 50 vouchers a jacket, and so on. Jokingly, at the end of the TV advert it said that for a million vouchers you could get a Harrier jump jet plane.

A couple of young guys in America decided to take that challenge seriously and, with the help of friends, eventually, collected the million vouchers. Imagine the surprise on the faces of the Pepsico executives when the two guys turned up with a million vouchers, asking for their Harrier jump jet! Pepsico said they were only joking on the advert, but the guys argued that if you are prepared to talk the talk then you also got to walk the walk. In their eyes, Pepsico had said something and were obliged to back it up by their actions.

I wouldn't be surprised to hear that the case still continues in court to this day. The point of me telling this story is that we have to be a generation of Christians who don't just make extravagant statements about life; we can back those statements up with what we actually do.

✉ FROM THE WEB ✉

'Just to say thanks IGNITE. You gave me the courage to talk about my faith and now two of my friends have become Christians – bargain! Jesus rules, baby!'

Step up where you are . . .

Many of you reading this might be thinking that in order to be a really effective evangelist or missionary you will have to travel to some far-flung part of the world to take the message of Jesus. If God is calling you to serve Him overseas, then go for it! But no one should miss out on the responsibility of stepping up to the microphone right where you are. In fact, when Jesus commissions the disciples He tells them to start in Jerusalem first. The evangelist, J. John, always says that a missionary isn't someone who crosses the sea, it's someone who sees the cross. The focus is on God's love, not necessarily on travelling. You could travel to the ends of the earth but it would be of no value unless you were consumed by the love of God.

✉ **FROM THE WEB** ✉

'Since I signed to IGNITE, five of my friends have given their lives to Jesus.'

. . . and step up where God sends you

Having said all of the above, there is a pressing need to take the message of Jesus to the ends of the earth. As part of the IGNITE initiative, we are excited about sending short-term mission teams out – particularly into schools in the UK, and into other countries where the need is great. Our first overseas mission team recently came back from Amsterdam. Working in partnership with a church, our team spent ten days sharing the love of God with children and teenagers on the streets of one of the most cosmopolitan and spiritually dark cities in the world. It was an experience that has changed our team members for ever. Having stepped up to the microphone overseas, they are much more aware of the need to do the same where they live.

There are many millions of people in this world who have never heard the name of Jesus, and there are friends of yours who have never heard who Jesus really is either. When we take mission teams into secondary schools we are constantly amazed at the ignorance about Jesus that we encounter. Many teenagers do not know the significance of the cross they wear as a fashion statement; many do not know the full story of Easter; most have a warped view of Christianity and church. Yet when we ask them, the majority of teenagers admit to a desire to knowing if there really is a God or not and to a yearning for love, acceptance and self-worth.

A large part of the IGNITE declaration is about growing a generation of disciples who will know the right way to go in life: they will show the way to others and they will go on that way with them. The Bible gives us five pictures to help us recognise how we can more effectively step up to the microphone and be powerful representatives for Jesus in the world we live in.

1. Witnesses

'But you will receive power when the Holy Spirit comes on you; and you will be my witnesses in Jerusalem, and in all Judea and Samaria, and to the ends of the earth.' (Acts 1:8)

In a church that I belonged to for many years there is a man called Alan Cowley. He used to be the church treasurer, but his job was a policeman in the South Wales constabulary. I will always remember asking Alan to share a few words with the congregation one Sunday morning about what made an effective witness from the point of view of the law. Alan was regularly required to take statements from witnesses and was often in court to give statements as a witness himself. What he said was incredibly helpful and made me realise just what God expects from you and me as witnesses. These were some of the points Alan Cowley highlighted:

● Good witnesses have something to tell.
● Good witnesses tell the truth.
● Good witnesses don't exaggerate.
● Good witnesses have characters that are authentic and honest.
● Good witnesses make the story most important, not themselves.
● Good witnesses have a real-life experience which

cannot be defeated by someone who merely has an argument.

See what I mean? That's the type of witness that you could be! Think about the man in John 9 who was blind. Jesus meets him by the pool of Siloam and cures him of his blindness by putting mud on his eyes. The man wipes the mud away and he can see. His neighbours are amazed by all this and quite naturally ask him what has been going on. He tells it just like it happened. Then the religious leaders get to hear what's been going on and they summon the man for questioning. Once again, he tells it as it was. Still not convinced, the religious leaders send for his parents to ask them what's been happening. The parents say that their son is old enough to speak for himself, so yet again the man gets the opportunity to tell what happened. My favourite verses from this story are these:

A second time they summoned the man who had been blind. 'Give glory to God,' they said. 'We know this man is a sinner.' He replied, 'Whether he is a sinner or not, I don't know. One thing I do know. I was blind but now I see!' (John 9:24)

Once he has responded in this way, all his opponents are dead and buried. However hard they try, and whatever tricky question they come up with, they can't dispute that the man is a witness to the fact that once he was blind but now he can see. Go and read the whole of the story for yourself.

2. Living letters

You yourselves are our letter, written on our hearts, known and read by everybody. You show that you are a letter from Christ, the result of our ministry, written not with ink but with the Spirit of the living God, not on tablets of stone but on tablets of human hearts. (2 Corinthians 3:2–3)

Jesus has sent you as a real-life letter to the people around you. Your most powerful opportunity to share the love of Jesus is when you step up to the microphone in front of your natural audience rather than searching for a contrived one.

One of life's little pleasures is coming down in the morning and collecting the mail from the doorstep. I get quite excited about a pile of letters, but often get disappointed by something that looks inviting on the envelope but is junk mail when I open it. On the other hand, receiving good news in a letter, something that is new and exciting, is great fun. Is your life a letter from Jesus that anyone can read just by looking at you? When they open up your envelope, are they disappointed at what they see inside, or is it really good news?

3. A sweet smell

> But thanks be to God, who always leads us in triumphal procession in Christ and through us spreads everywhere the fragrance of the knowledge of him. For we are to God the aroma of Christ among those who are being saved and those who are perishing. To the one we are the smell of death; to the other, the fragrance of life. And who is equal to such a task? (2 Corinthians 2:14–16)

Just one flower can fill a room with a pleasant aroma. Just one splash of perfume can transform a person's smell. This passage suggests that you should give off a sweet smell that sends people sniffing after the source – and that's Jesus. The stark reality is that sometimes we have got spiritual BO because our walk with God isn't always fresh. So don't go stale; keep fresh, and be the aroma of Christ.

4. Shining stars

> 'You are the light of the world. A city on a hill cannot be hidden. Neither do people light a lamp and put it under a bowl. Instead they put it on its stand, and it gives light to everyone in the house. In the same way, let your light shine before men, that they may see your good deeds and praise your Father in heaven.' (Matthew 5:14–16)

I must have heard the Newsboys sing 'Step Up to the Microphone' about 60 times, but I reckon I have heard them sing their song 'Shine' nearly 200 times! In fact, I don't think I've seen them perform live when they haven't sung 'Shine'. The chorus sums up what being a shining star is all about:

> Shine
> Make 'em wonder what you've got
> Make 'em wish that they were not
> On the outside looking bored
> Shine
> Let it shine before all men
> Let 'em see good works.
> And then
> Let 'em glorify the Lord

> (Lyrics by Steve Taylor ©1994 Ariose Music,
> admin. by EMI Christian music publishing.)

I hope you get the message! When people look at you they should see Jesus as clearly as if they were looking at a lighthouse shining out on a dark night. People are attracted by light, and more often than not it's difficult to go in the opposite direction.

Once on an adventure day in the Brecon Beacons I was lowered down a silica mine shaft on a rope. My instructions were to reach the bottom and then turn away from what little light I could see and walk into the pitch black. If I walked towards the light I would fall into a very deep hole, so I had to stumble in the darkness for a few minutes until I saw another light, and then follow that. Walking away from the first light was a very scary experience. If people can see in you a shining light they will naturally be attracted rather than walking away.

5. A new kind of fisherman

The disciples' response to the invitation by Jesus to 'Come, follow me' was to leave behind one life and start a new one. They would have had some idea, as their journey with Jesus progressed, why he chose to say they would be fishers of men. Fish, nets, bait, catches, and all the hard work, experience and commitment that fishing entailed, were familiar parts of their lives.

You need to apply the same criteria to your life. How should you adjust your net to catch more people up in God's love? What bait should you use? Where should you fish? Whose lives do you most want to catch? How much hard work are you prepared to put in?

In the summer, my daughter Bethan and I love to go down to the beach and wander around the rock pools for hours on end. Our aim is a simple one – to catch as many crabs or tiddlers as we can (we always put them straight back). You can't imagine the thrill we get when we manage to catch a fish, because they usually dart around so quickly. We take our nets and our buckets, turn over all the rocks we can manage to lift, and will happily spend all afternoon in pursuit of a big'un (he'll probably only be an inch or so long!). The determination and persistence of real fishermen should be your inspiration to be fishers of men.

REAL-LIFE STORY

Lois Richards is a 16-year-old A level student from Merthyr Tydfil and a volunteer with Big Ideas.

'At Spring Harvest in 1999, Dawn Reynolds, a well-known female speaker, spent some time with me, and having discovered my passions she said she felt I was going to be an evangelist. I was only 14 at the time and was pretty scared. My initial thought was that this was SO not me and to be honest I was overwhelmed. For example, what was that going to mean for the rest of my life?

'Very soon I realised that it wasn't just about the future but also about how I lived my life day-to-day right now, especially at school. A few months later, at a conference called Flames of Fire, at the Royal Welsh Showground, Nigel James prayed for two of us (me and a girl called Fiona from North Wales). It was as if Nigel was commissioning us as we responded to God's call to be evangelists. Some of the specific things Nigel prayed were confirmation to me, because I hadn't spoken to anyone about what Dawn Reynolds had said.

'In the following November my class was doing a GCSE speaking and listening exercise. I asked God what I should speak about and He replied, "Lois, you've got to speak about me." I really, really didn't want to do it but I knew I had to

and that it was going to be a major step of faith. My friends knew I was a Christian because I hadn't exactly been quiet about it, but speaking in front of the whole class was going to be a big challenge.

'My turn to speak came directly after a guy who spoke about evolution and why he believed God didn't exist! I got up and can't really remember what I said, other than being really passionate about Jesus and really going for it. My basic message was, "Look guys, God is real and he really loves you." I felt so led by the Holy Spirit and God anointed me. It was as if He was saying to me, "Now you've stood up and given me the chance, I'm going to do all the work you thought was so scary." As soon as I sat down, I knew that life would need to be different; I would need to be an example of what I spoke about. It wasn't just the words I was going to say, but I had to live the life too.

'A few more months after that lesson, two of my friends became Christians. Basically, they had both been dissing church but thought they couldn't keep doing that in front of me until they'd tried it out for themselves. So they started coming to church with me and to IGNITE evenings also. One became a Christian at an IGNITE event, and the other became a Christian in my bedroom when we read and prayed through "Three Simple Words to Change Your Life", which is a gospel leaflet produced by Big Ideas.

'I don't want anyone to get the idea that it's been all lovey-dovey, fine and lush since I stood up in front of the class, because it hasn't been. There have already been some very hard times, but God has been with me in the pants times and the wicked lush times too. People at school do notice me living a different life to them, one that strives to be pure, and incredibly they do see Jesus in me! They talk to me about the difficult stuff they are going through and the problems they are facing. They see that I am facing some of the same issues as them and that I rely on God to help me. One of the things that I also want to get across to my friends is that I am there for them whether they are Christians or not. I believe that is the type of love that Jesus showed.

'One of the things I'm learning about being an evangelist is that it isn't necessarily about standing on a big stage, although Big Ideas have given me some opportunities to do that. It's just as important how you live your everyday life. What has really helped me is reading the Bible – it's my source for the stuff I talk to people about. Jesus wants us to tell everyone about Him and all of us should strive to live a life that is more like Jesus.

'The IGNITE declaration has helped me to be more bold and to live out my passion for seeing my friends meet Jesus and see Him heal the pain that so many young people have. I'm totally up for it, to weep for my friends, to have my heart broken for them and not just witnessing to them because someone has told me it's the right thing to do.

'The evenings that IGNITE put on are such blatant opportunities to bring my friends into an environment that isn't boring, and that I'm not embarrassed about. It's a totally funky and welcoming vibe and a place to experience God's love and see who Jesus is and why he loves them.

'I'm 16 now, but I pray that when I'm 26 I'll still have the same passion to be holy, pure and honest. I want to be sharing Jesus with young people but also with my contemporaries as well. I'm really challenged by the words of Jesus at the end of Matthew's Gospel. I want to be part of His plan to go out and spread the Word and I know that Jesus will always be with me. One of my role models would be Esther – I just love her story in the Old Testament. She stood up for her people in hard times and against persecution, and she did it all as a woman in a male-dominated culture. That rocks!'

❗ IGNITE DECLARATION ❗

Take the message of Jesus into my school, college or place of work and the world by praying, living and witnessing so that everyone may have an opportunity to know Jesus.

🔥 FIRESTARTERS 🔥

- Read the story of the healing of the blind man in John 9.
- What lessons about being a witness can you learn from that story?
- Start talking naturally to a Christian friend about what God has been doing in your life recently.
- Start talking naturally to a friend who isn't a Christian about what God has been doing in your life recently.

- Ask God to reveal to you three non-Christian friends who you should pray for regularly.
- Ask God to reveal to you the areas of your life that He needs to change so that you can 'step up to the microphone' more effectively.
- Ask God to give you a heart that learns to love lost people who don't know Jesus.

8
big ideas

✉ **FROM THE WEB** ✉

'Just wanted to tell you that I've been really touched recently by the importance and effectiveness of prayer. God has amazing plans for us all. It's a matter of being expectant and willing to sacrifice so that His will may be done through us.'

One of the most exciting and scary times of my life was when I began to realise that God was calling me to take a step of faith into something new. You'll find the details of that in this chapter's Real-Life Story. Something new eventually became the charity Big Ideas, which itself gave birth to the IGNITE initiative.

I remember a time when Gary Smith and I were

invited to be consultants to a group of Methodist churches just outside Cardiff. The minister of the churches was a man called John Haley who was a long-time friend. John wanted us to act as evangelism consultants and trainers for his Methodist churches. One evening, we were meeting representatives of the various churches and sharing our vision with them. One lady came out with a classic line. She said, 'I don't think we are ready for Big Ideas; we need some little ideas, or perhaps some medium-sized ideas, but definitely not big ones.' I had to tell her that the name of our charity was non-negotiable and that she was stuck with Big Ideas.

Yet her comments did make me think. More than one person has said to us that the name Big Ideas is a bold and even arrogant one. In America, people often meet Gary and me with the comment, 'Hey guys, what's the big idea?' and then laugh as if they are the only person who has ever said it to us! Gary came up with the name Big Ideas from an old song by veteran Christian singer Randy Stonehill, and we have never seen the name as anything but reflecting the BIG IDEAS God has for me and you and the rest of this world.

You see, if you think that God only has small ideas for you, or at best medium-sized ones, then think again, because God's plan for this world he created, you included, is a massive one. The challenge of this chapter is to discover God's will and to continue exploring it with everything you have got.

I must admit that there have been times in my life when I wished God would shout out loud His plans for me, or send me a personal letter explaining exactly what it was He wanted me to do. Neither of those things have really happened, not even when we started Big Ideas. Yet there have been some consistent ways that I have discovered God's will for my life, and this chapter explains five of them.

1. Don't be fooled by your appearance

Years and years ago there used to be a slogan that said 'Be patient – God hasn't finished with me yet'. There is a lot of truth in that. God is still at work in your life and in many ways you and I aren't the finished article. That means we will still make mistakes and will still have some rough edges. Now listen carefully: I'm not saying this so that you have an excuse for failure, bad behaviour and sinfulness, but I am saying if you ever get really down on yourself and you feel you have really blown it, just remember that God still has plenty more to do in your life if you will let Him. Even the apostle Paul recognised that he was far from the finished article: 'What a wretched man I am! Who will rescue me from this body of death?' (Romans 7:24)

Sometimes you might look at Christian leaders and wish that you could be like them. In my travels on the road with Christian bands and solo artists, I frequently come across fans who have a completely unrealistic and idealistic view of their heroes. I'm often told by a forlorn fan: 'If only I could be like so and so, he's a really awesome man of God.' The truth of the situation is that the public figures you see only show you their public side and so you don't realise they face many of the same struggles that you do!

God can change lives! Perhaps you already know that and have experienced it, but God wants to do something new in YOUR life. He's given you a new heart; He wants to build you a new character and He gives you a new power to live by.

So don't be fooled by the way you see yourself at the moment – whether you think you are the greatest person who ever lived or whether you think you are a miserable worm. See yourself the way God sees you: perfectly loved, with immeasurable potential and destined to become more and more like Jesus.

2. Discover yourself in the Bible

We live in a world where people go to great lengths to 'find themselves'. Out-of-favour pop stars attempt to reinvent themselves; TV shows create makeovers for men and women who aren't happy with who they are. You will never find yourself more completely than by being the person God made you to be.

One of the most helpful hints for reading the Bible I have ever been told is to find the characters in Scripture that you match. In fact, I've taken it one stage further. When I read words that Jesus speaks to the disciples, I believe He is speaking them to me. You see, God believes in you just as he believed in all the inadequate, unreliable, inexperienced characters in the Bible who eventually came good! How about Jonah, for example?

Jonah runs away from the call of God to start with, and soon finds himself in the belly of a whale! Yet God gives him another chance. Even then, Jonah has a disagreement with God and thinks he knows better than the Lord himself. (Check out the story in the book of Jonah in your Bible.)

Our image of the superheroes of the Bible often needs to be adjusted when we see that they were far from perfect yet were still used by God. I often return to the story of Simon Peter. He comes across Jesus in Luke 5 and initially feels he is not worthy even to meet Jesus. Soon Jesus tells him he's going to be a fisher of men. Peter was a fisherman and so knew all about nets, boats and catches of fish. But Jesus is thinking in different terms. He was seeing that Peter would have an incredible impact into people's lives.

Friends of Peter might have predicted his foolish attempt to walk on water (who else other than Jesus managed a step or two?), and they might have known he would lose his temper and cut the ear off the High

Priest's servant. They would have laughed at his bravado when he told Jesus that he would never disown Him, and then they would have winced when he denied Christ three times.

Yet Jesus saw past all of that and saw a character that would mature. He saw a man who was going to preach to the crowd on the Day of Pentecost, a man who would heal a blind beggar, who would be flogged by the Sanhedrin, who was instrumental in the good news of Jesus spreading to the Gentiles, a man who had visions from God, who escaped from prison, who wrote two letters included in the New Testament and who was eventually crucified himself. Legend has it that he was crucified upside down because he felt himself unworthy to be crucified in the same way as Jesus.

So go on and find yourself in the Bible: let God speak to you through it as you let the Holy Spirit be your guide.

3. Go against the flow

The reality of Christian living is that you must travel in the opposite direction to what many would consider worldly success. When Jesus gave the disciples the option of following Him he said they would need to take up their cross. Imagine you were a disciple and Jesus was speaking to you. What would be going through your mind when He told you to take up your cross? You wouldn't have known about Jesus' own crucifixion yet, but the image of a cross would be a hauntingly familiar one to you. You would have seen criminals bent double under the weight of the cross as they carried it to their own execution. They would have seen those criminals hanging on the cross on a distant hill.

It's that type of life Jesus is calling you to. A life so committed to Him and to self-sacrifice that you won't mind being different; you'll rely on the power of God to help you go one way when everyone else is trying to persuade you to go their way. Going against the flow means having a different set of attitudes, thoughts and a different world-view than the majority of people in life. Be encouraged, though – more and more folk in this world are deciding to follow Jesus and go against the flow.

The IGNITE declaration will give you a great focus as you decide to be different. Remember that as you go against the flow not only are you being obedient to God but Jesus travels with you. In John 17 Jesus talks much about the 'world' and is at pains to explain that if you really consider yourself a follower of His you will not feel totally at ease in this world because you really belong to another kingdom. In his writing, the apostle Paul expands this even further and explains that even our values, thoughts and perceived wisdom must be turned upside down (remember when we were looking at including Jesus in our thoughts?):

For the foolishness of God is wiser than man's wisdom, and the weakness of God is stronger than man's strength. Brothers, think of what you were when you were called. Not many of you were wise by human standards; not many were influential; not many were of noble birth. But God chose the foolish things of the world to shame the wise; God chose the weak things of the world to shame the strong. (1 Corinthians 1:25–28)

4. Enter the marathon not the sprint

In the Mexico Olympics of 1968, a runner called John Akhwari ran the marathon and finished over an hour after the winner. When he entered the stadium it was virtually empty. Someone asked him why he didn't just give up and catch the bus back to the Olympic village. Akhwari replied: 'My country did not send me 10,000 kilometres to start the race; they sent me 10,000 kilometres to finish the race.'

There is a famous saying that sums up Akhwari's feelings: 'Success lies not in what you start but in what you finish.' This sentiment can be found in Scripture too. Here is Paul speaking again:

However, I consider my life worth nothing to me, if only I may finish the race and complete the task the Lord Jesus has given me – the task of testifying to the gospel of God's grace. (Acts 20:24)

Never believe that conversion is the end of what God wants to do in your life. Never believe that you won't face tough times. Always pray to God for strength, determination and perseverance to finish the race He is putting in front of you. Stay in it for the long haul – it won't be a short sprint of initial energy; it will need to be the marathon. Don't worry if others seem to be running stronger or faster than you – the deal is to win the solo race you are in, not to compete against anyone else.

5. Get involved

The Message translation of the Bible puts Ephesians 4:2 like this: 'I want you to get out there and walk – better yet, run! – on the road God called you to travel. I don't want any of you sitting around on your hands.'

I went to a rugby playing school, which for someone like me, who loved football, was a bit of a struggle. I would get put in the scrum every week and can still hear the games master bellowing 'GET STUCK IN' to all of us who spent the match close to the touch-line, almost as spectators. I must admit that since then I've grown to realise the frustrations of having people on a team who would rather watch than get involved.

The story is told of the American, General Patton, in the Second World War. He would frequently go up to his troops and ask the question, 'What is your mission?'

The soldiers were in big trouble if they didn't answer. We are all involved in God's mission to save mankind, and I hope by now that even if you haven't found your place in that mission this book will have at least given you some guidance as to how to discover your place.

In John 6 the disciples see the feeding of 5,000 men unfold before them. When you read the story you see that actually they were involved in the miracle taking shape. Although Jesus did the miraculous with the loaves and fish, it was the disciples who found the bread and fish, brought it to Jesus, handed it out to the crowd and collected up the leftovers. Even a young boy was involved – he was the one who had the foresight to bring five loaves and two fish in the first place, and he was willing to hand them over!

When you discover your place in the body of Christ you will have a part to play. You'll be blessed yourself and you'll be a blessing to others. Following Jesus means your life will count.

I don't believe that God has a ready-prepared route for you on your journey – only the final destination is a certainty. Although He has plans for you, your free will means you have some optional directions on the way. Many Christians would like to be completely controlled by God, as if they were a robot with no mind or choice of their own. I'm not encouraging rebellion here at all, just pointing out that to a certain extent God calls you to use the self-control he has given you in order to make decisions and guide your life. Part of that self-discipline is to submit your own will to God's will.

Look at the first verse of most of Paul's letters – he tells us he is an apostle *by the will of God*. Even Jesus himself, before the crucifixion, says to God, *'Not my will but yours be done.'*

So discover God's will for your life and pursue it with every breath that you take. Paul, in his conversion vision in Acts 9, is told by Jesus: 'Now get up and go into the city, and you will be told what you must do' (Acts 9:6).

Towards the end of the book of Acts, Paul is facing trial in front of Agrippa and he recalls his conversion and particularly the vision:

> Then I asked, 'Who are you, Lord?' 'I am Jesus, whom you are persecuting,' the Lord replied. 'Now get up and stand on your feet. I have appeared to you to appoint you as a servant and as a witness of what you have seen of me and what I will show you. I will rescue you from your own people and from the Gentiles. I am sending you to them to open their eyes and turn them from darkness to light, and from the power of Satan to God, so that they may receive forgiveness of sins and a place among those who are sanctified by faith in me.' So then, King Agrippa, I was not disobedient to the vision from heaven. (Acts 26:15–19)

That's the kind of obedience to His will that God wants from you!

REAL-LIFE STORY

Gary Smith is a director of Big Ideas, along with his brother-in-law Nigel James.

'I was born in 1962 and was part of the last generation that was encouraged to go to Sunday school. I went down to the parish hall each Sunday morning and can never remember a time when I didn't believe in the existence of God or the truth of Jesus, but these things didn't really impact my life in any deep way.

'I moved over to a Methodist church after a while because they had a youth club, and then I joined The Boys' Brigade. Christian faith is an intrinsic part of the B.B., and I was interested in the faith stuff: in fact, I could talk about the religious side of things with some clarity, but this had little effect on my decision-making or wider thinking.

'I left school at the age of 16, with spectacularly unsuccessful examination results, which were a disappointment to my school and to my parents, and a shock to me. So I went out and got a job, mainly to be independent and to earn some money. Moving from job to job, I eventually found one as a trainee recruitment consultant in the I.T. industry. This job went well, then very well, and before too long I was earning a huge salary with bonuses and other fringe benefits.

'My plan for independence and money was taking shape, but at the same time I had stayed involved with The Boys' Brigade and had begun to mix with young people from all

over the UK. These young people clearly had something I didn't. Sharing with them at conferences and residential weekends I began to see that Jesus really did make a difference in their lives and in their decision-making. The realisation that I needed to know Jesus, not just know about Him, and that I needed to know Him intimately, just would not go away. This became a major quest in my life, and successful as I was at work (at one stage having two company cars on my drive!) the real buzz I got was from being in a Christian environment and spending time with people who were on fire for God. I began to pray that I would become like them and be more passionate about Jesus, and I desperately wanted Jesus to impact my life the way He was impacting others.

'My first clear sense of calling from God was when I knew that I must step out from the successful and financially rewarding job I was doing and begin to serve God much more directly than I had been. Looking back, I can remember hearing that calling from God in a variety of ways. First, there was a growing sense inside me that I needed to give my life, both personally and professionally, completely over to God. Second, people I valued and trusted began to discuss regularly with me that I could live my life in a way that glorified God. Third, I had achieved everything that I had assumed would label me successful – the job, the cars, the salary, my own house – yet still found little fulfilment. In fact, as I read the Bible around this time I came across the story of the foolishness of the farmer, in Luke's Gospel, who was building barns and bigger barns to store his crops. In the story, he died the very

same night that he was congratulating himself on his success. The heading for this story in my Bible was 'the rich fool' – and it had a powerful impact on me: not that I feared for my life, but I realised the futility of the life I was leading.

'As a result of all of this I decided to apply for a variety of jobs with a Christian flavour. People who didn't know me quite so well thought I would never move away from such a lucrative job; little did they know my growing conviction that a big salary was much less important than seeing people's lives changed. Of all the jobs that I applied for, only the B.B. interviewed me – for two possible positions: one I was very interested in, and one I didn't think would be so suitable. It was then that I believe God spoke to me in a fourth way. The Boys' Brigade offered me the job I was less keen on, so I prayed about it and left a decision overnight. I woke up the next morning with a certainty that this was the direction God wanted me to take, so I accepted the job.

'With such a clear sense of God's plan, it was easy to go to my old employers and hand my notice in, even when they offered to double my salary if I stayed.

'I worked for the B.B. for six years or so, and it was here that my friendship with Nigel really grew. We spent more and more time together working on evangelism and discipleship projects. Despite him being based in Cardiff and me being based in East Anglia, we developed a friendship and a mutual desire to serve God. For a couple of summers we toured B.B. campsites all over England and Wales with an evangelistic roadshow team; we helped the B.B. develop the Firm

Foundations Christian arts and teaching festival, and I pioneered a music and drama presentation, called *Firemaster*, which toured around East Anglia initially, then all over the UK.

'It was during this time that Nigel and I met many people from other Christian agencies and ministries and were further challenged by God. We both felt the urgency that God required of us, and although we tried a number of ways of remaining with The Boys' Brigade, we knew it was time to move on. After talking and praying together regularly, seeing God's hand on the gospel projects we had already undertaken, and consulting loads of friends, we realised God was demanding that we took a fresh step of faith into something new. So once again I left behind a salary and a car (although both were modest by previous comparisons) and along with Nigel established Big Ideas. I'd spent a fair bit of my life explaining to family members about my faith, so telling them about this new venture wasn't difficult. Telling my wife, Nigel's sister, wasn't too hard either – in fact, we had great support from our wives. The most difficult part was telling other Christians who didn't share our vision. Most needed convincing on one of two things – we weren't out to make loads of money, and we weren't about to bankrupt ourselves or our wives!

'I must admit that a real issue for me at the time was looking at other people who were so-called 'full-time Christians' and feeling very inadequate by comparison. Through the Firm Foundations festival we got to know folk like Dave Pope and Duncan Banks, John Peebles, Carl

McGregor, Steve Connor and Andy Harsant very well. Their names may or may not mean something to you, but through them and people like them I saw that God could take hold of ordinary people like me, with the same struggles that I had, and still do great things.

'In the first couple of years in the life of Big Ideas, Nigel and I literally went anywhere and did anything to explore relevant ways of communicating the Christian faith. During this time we began to discover and define more closely exactly what each of us should be doing. Christian music had always impacted my life, and having had a taster of being involved with it from the Firm Foundations festival, I really wanted to stay involved. Yet being a new ministry, with few contacts and little finance, the likelihood of working in the Christian music scene seemed slim.

'Before too long, God had incredibly opened doors and we were entering in a relationship with a Christian record company and working on their behalf in a number of projects. Nigel spent a week in the UK and Europe with Newsboys – the first time he had met them – and I began developing some large concerts for US and UK bands. Then Nigel and I found ourselves on an all-expenses-paid trip to Nashville for the annual meeting of the Gospel Music Association.

'I can clearly remember us sitting in the Ryman Auditorium (the home of the Grand Ole Opry) for a Sunday evening service, and through the preaching and ministry knowing that this was the right place for us to be spiritually, and that under the umbrella of Big Ideas our ministries were going to diversify. We had sufficient faith in God and in each other to believe that I should continue to develop opportunities in Christian music while Nigel should continue as a speaker and running missions. These decisions were quite tough in a way, but we recognised the signs God was giving us – not least that inner sense again of what we should be doing.

'Only a year ago, however, I had to have a major re-evaluation of my role, and needed to confirm that I was still travelling in the direction God wanted me to. Work had become so busy and manic, and I had ended up doing stuff and taking projects on board that were more functional than real priority. I was doing things purely because of our relationship with the record company, rather than from a sense of God's leading. Through a variety of circumstances, some of which were quite painful, God created space and opportunity for me to be much more focused on IGNITE.

'I've always seen my life as a Christian being about a journey, and I've been determined to see that journey as one of discovery and exploration. I believe all of us should never stop exploring how God wants us to be, and discovering new challenges and directions that he puts before us.'

IGNITE DECLARATION

I commit to: Explore God's will for myself and my generation and seek to follow it.

FIRESTARTERS

Use the following to help you know God's will:

- The word of God.
- Answered prayer.
- A sense of peace in your heart and mind.
- Guidance of other Christians.
- Opportunities that are open or shut to you.
- Common sense that God has given you.
- Spiritual gifts – words of knowledge or prophecy spoken over you.
- Visions or dreams that God gives you.

further info

IGNITE is a discipleship declaration and initiative that has sprung up from the Cardiff-based ministry Big Ideas. Launched in September 2000, IGNITE reached 1,000 sign-ups by Christmas 2001. In the early months of 2002, Big Ideas launched IGNITE around the UK, offering the declaration and various resources, such as this book, to churches and youth leaders that wanted to encourage young people in their locality to take seriously the challenge of living as a disciple of Jesus.

Big Ideas carries out a variety of evangelism and discipleship strategies, including regular IGNITE events in Cardiff. These range from worship and teaching evenings to evangelistic events that young Christians can bring their friends to. As well as IGNITE events, Big Ideas regularly works in school R.E. departments in

Cardiff and often puts teams together to work in schools around the UK. Another aspect of the work of Big Ideas has been to create platforms for Christian artists to perform around the UK and in Europe. To that end, Big Ideas has regularly partnered with Rebecca St James, Eli, Newsboys and Chris Eaton, and has also worked with DC Talk, Delirious, Switchfoot, Sarah Masen, All Star United, The W's, Jeni Varnadeau, Steve Apirana, World Wide Message Tribe, and many more.

Increasingly, though, Big Ideas is making a priority of helping the young people of churches in and around Cardiff discover a passion for serving Jesus. It is from this heart that IGNITE has been born. Young people are joining IGNITE short-term mission teams from Big Ideas to serve their generation around the UK and overseas.

To discover more about IGNITE and the declaration, resources, merchandise and mission teams, check out the website www.igniteme.org

Youth leaders can visit the specific page on the IGNITE website for youth leaders, and will receive a password for regular visits to enable them to discover teaching material and articles designed to help them in youth ministry.

To contact Nigel James personally you can email him at nigel@igniteme.org

To discover more about the overall ministry of Big Ideas, IGNITE, or to invite Nigel James to speak at your church or youth event, then use any of the following contact points:

Big Ideas
PO Box 39
PENARTH
CF64 2YH
S. Wales

Phone: 02920 811441
Fax: 02920 811341
Email: info@bigideas.org.uk

The Unquenchable Worshipper

by Matt Redman

This book is about a kind of worshipper:

Unquenchable. Undivided. Unpredictable.

On a quest to bring glory and pleasure to God, these worshippers will not allow themselves to be distracted or defeated:

Unstoppable. Undignified. Undone.

Worshippers who long for their hearts, lives and songs to be the kind of offerings God is looking for.

'This is unashamedly a book about God and living a devoted life in His presence. Worship is *about* God, *to* God and *for* God. *The Unquenchable Worshipper* shouts this truth out loud.'

Mike Pilavachi, Soul Survivor

survivor

GREAT IDEAS

50 Ways to help Your Church Grow
David Beer
'Wonderfully practical and inspiring'
— RICK WARREN
author of 'The Purpose-Driven Church'
FOREWORD BY STEVE CHALKE

50 Easy Outreach Ideas
Bringing church and community together
Paul Mogford

100 Instant Discussion Starters
Guaranteed to get your group talking!
John Buckeridge

100 Talks for Parents
Outlines for Parent & Toddler Groups
Fiona Castle and Joyce Gledhill

25 Sketches about Proverbs
David Burt
Bringing Biblical proverbs to life through drama

50 Sketches about Jesus
David Burt
'A bumper bran-tub of breezy curtain-raisers'
— PAUL BURBRIDGE
Riding Lights Theatre Company

50 Worship Ideas for Small Groups
Stuart Townend
with Morgan Lewis

Helping You to Help Others